AGAINST SACRIFICE

AGAINST SACRIFICE

AN ESSAY ON RISK AND ETHICS

HENRY P WYNN

Matador
9 Priory Business Park,
Wistow Road, Kibworth Beauchamp,
Leicestershire. LE8 0RX
Tel: 0116 279 2299
Email: books@troubador.co.uk
Web: www.troubador.co.uk/matador
Twitter: @matadorbooks

ISBN 978 1800463 363

British Library Cataloguing in Publication Data.
A catalogue record for this book is available from the British Library.

Printed and bound in Great Britain by 4edge Limited
Typeset in 10pt Minion Pro by Troubador Publishing Ltd, Leicester, UK

Matador is an imprint of Troubador Publishing Ltd

Contents

Preface

This book arose out a thought I had at some risk conference, somewhere, when I realised that the unquestioning use of utility would lead to the sacrifice of some lives for others. The idea then was probably quite technical, such as whether early participants in clinical trials were at greater risk than latter entrants or that people were sacrificed today to save people tomorrow. It then just spread out in different directions mopping up even older concerns of mine such as blaming the victim and collateral damage. This essay is the result and it is a sad irony it has particular relevance to the COVID-19 and climate change crises. Not being a professional ethicist, it was hard work for me, although here and there I may pull rank in statistics and risk.

My soul sister and wife Jan Baldwin gets most of the thanks for her huge insight, continuous moral support and infinite patience. Peter Abell, friend and LSE co-Emeritus, from whom I have learned swathes of economic and political philosophy, also gets a big slice of gratitude.

This book is dedicated to my late brother Stephen Wynn whose phrase "they are not doing their job", reflecting his single handed battles with regulators, inspires the last chapter.

Special thanks to Ros Byam Shaw for an early and very useful proofread.

1.

Not in peacetime

I see the Four-fold Man, The Humanity in deadly sleep
And its fallen Emanation, the Spectre and its cruel Shadow.
I see the Past, Present and Future existing all at once
Before me. O Divine Spirit, sustain me on thy wings,
That I may awake Albion from his long and cold repose;
For Bacon and Newton, sheath'd in dismal steel, their terrors hang
Like iron scourges over Albion: reasonings like vast serpents
Infold around my limbs, bruising my minute articulations.

I turn my eyes to the schools and universities of Europe
And there behold the Loom of Locke, whose Woof rages dire,
Wash'd by the Water-wheels of Newton: black the cloth
In heavy wreaths folds over every nation: cruel works
Of many Wheels I view, wheel without wheel, with cogs tyrannic
Moving by compulsion each other, not as those in Eden, which,
Wheel within wheel, in freedom revolve in harmony and peace.

William Blake [1]

Commanders in wartime may have to make difficult decisions in which one group of soldiers is sacrificed to protect another, or a sacrifice may be made within a group, where some soldiers are killed and others survive. The objective is to defeat the enemy; in which case, such events and their dilemmas can be seen as part of a wider discussion about just or unjust wars, which may also include moral issues about attacks on civilians. My main purpose in this essay is to elaborate on the simple idea that, in the long-term strategic or day-to-day operational decision-making of organisations and governments in peacetime, the sacrifice of one group to save another is not legitimate or at least should have very strict limits. The style and moral basis of decision-making in wartime are fundamentally not applicable in peacetime.

Despite my emphasis on civil society, there is a chapter on drone warfare where the contrast with peacetime is visceral. Collateral damage, in a broad sense, occurs in both peace and war as a result of administrative action. I will show that, despite their inapplicability, the dubious and outdated moralities of war continue to cast shadows on civilian life. The concepts of "proportionality", "acceptability" and "necessity" are prime examples.

I shall describe how – in modern, liberal, Western democracies – sacrifices are made and made routinely, often in secret, with no clear limits and with no proper representation of the sacrificed. Where there are committees or special bodies to discuss, advise or take decisions on matters that affect human life, they are often appointed and not elected, while their terms of reference may enshrine the notion of sacrifice in a covert way.

This is all about ethics, but there is insufficient ethical debate in public life about these matters. When analysed, the decision-making is often grounded on an outdated type of ethics – a nineteenth-century, utilitarian way of thinking that is given an additional boost from twentieth-century mathematical economics: utility, rational choice, profit and loss, cost-benefit analysis and so on. Mixed in with this are a few extra spices borrowed from the ethics of war. The celebrity chef of this unpalatable soup is Margaret Thatcher, with her often quoted phrase "there must be winners and losers". It is usually the powerful who tell us there have to be trade-offs, just as they say we all have to make sacrifices in wartime.

The economists, in their own defence, will argue that we need not be too concerned because all these issues are well covered by areas such as welfare economics and theories of choice, and that a little more theory will sort it all out. By allowing better mathematical definitions of utility, choice and welfare, they will say that we can get a grip on topics such as inequality, which they may tell us is what we are really talking about. However, these experts never really mention the sacrificed and certainly do not side with them. They are brushed aside with euphemistic terms such as "negative externalities". They will argue that the pursuit of profit, the generation of wealth, and the stabilisation of supply and demand may require both the maximisation of value and the optimisation of some technical and management processes. But in matters of sickness and health, and in the welfare of the young and old, such raw calculation naturally leads to sacrifice and, I shall argue, is fundamentally not valid and *not acceptable*.

At their most brutal, these utilitarian approaches lead to a direct translation of life into cash via the Orwellian concept of quality-of-life indices or quality-adjusted life years (QALYs). These have a foothold in universities under the banner of "health economics". There are scores of postgraduate courses in this area in the UK, and many experts, some of whom act as advisors for the government. Health economics hopes to answer questions, or at least do the calculations to help others answer questions, such as who do we keep alive: a productive parent of thirty or a sick grandmother of ninety-two?

Modern ethical theory and its Cinderella sub-area, applied ethics, covers some of this ground, but the concept of sacrifice is rarely mentioned. In a review of twenty well-known books on ethics that I have to hand, none has the word "sacrifice" or the word "victim" in the index. But it stalks the pages. John Rawls, in particular, challenges the raw, utilitarian approach and advocates a maximin approach: maximise the position of the worst off.[2] At the other end of the avenue, Robert Nozick uses "no sacrifice" as a driving argument, but it is an entirely different concept of sacrifice to ours.[3] He is concerned to say that the rich paying more tax is a sacrifice for them. He uses it to support a rightist view of ethics, which is so strident that it drives him in some logical way, with his libertarian comrades, towards the advocacy of a minimal state.

If there is sacrifice of life without representation, then our government should not be surprised if the family and friends of the sacrificed take some kind of political action. It is surely understandable for people to ask "Why me?" or "Why my grandmother?". In wartime, refusals to be sacrificed in the face of the enemy have led to soldiers being shot for cowardice. We do not shoot people in peacetime, at least not in the UK. However, life can be made difficult for the refuseniks when they appear to go against the public good.

The decisions that governments have to take are becoming more and more complex, with the cost of error probably greater than at any previous time in history. Consider the list: climate change, terrorism, pandemics, species diversity, weapons of mass destruction and many more. In addition to coping with these global phenomena, governments are held responsible for the domestic economy, health, education, transport, defence, and law and order. Who would be a politician? They are caught between the demands of a sceptical public and the modern corporate bulldozers of globalisation. Faced with this, it is hardly surprising that they surround themselves with civil servants, experts, advisors, working parties, commissions (in the UK these are sometimes "royal"), boards, agencies and regulatory authorities. The UK is running short of three-letter acronyms and initialisms. At one time, the name "FSA" referred to both the Financial Services Authority and the Food Standards Agency. (Try to work out the difference between an agency and an authority.)

What are the rules? Person or body A appoints person B to committee C, which has terms of reference D. If we joined the A, B, C and D on a big chart and hung it on the wall, we would have an interesting snapshot of modern Britain. We could create a whole network to see who is on more than one node, and inspect it for diversity. "Lay" is an interesting word. Originally meaning non-clerical, it has come to mean non-professional or Joe Public. If the definition is not too murky, then we could invent a "lay index", such as the percentage of lay people on a committee. Interesting patterns might emerge, and we could even study the system dynamically over time as members of committees come and go. We should add all the more permanent arm's length bodies (ALBs), which in the UK number over 450, spend £20 billion a year of public funds, and have only a skeleton level of accountability, which is something that concerns a number of select committees of Parliament.[4] What happened to the good old QUANGO (the quasi-autonomous non-governmental organisation), when did a QUANGO change into an ALB, and what is the lay index for ALBs? And so on. This would be a nice topic for a master's dissertation or PhD thesis, if it hasn't already been written.

But the complex geometry of public life takes a more human and urgent quality if we pin a red flag to any committee on our chart where decisions are taken that affect life and death, and which may lead to the sacrifice of one group of people for the benefit of another. Every week in some group, somewhere, ethical positions are taken, where the word "ethics" may seldom be used and the word "sacrifice" never. One can respect the seriousness, the professional expertise and the responsibility shown, but not the secrecy, the lack of public debate and the sometimes-only-cursory accountability. One might call this fog-like reticence "the cowardice of the politicians". I shall discuss secrecy later.

We need to be very careful about such committees. Their possible existence has been used by libertarians to attack the state. Here is a statement by Sarah Palin:

> *Government healthcare will not reduce the cost; it will simply refuse to pay the cost. And who will suffer the most when they ration care? The sick, the elderly, and the disabled, of course. The America I know and love is not one in which my parents or my baby with Down Syndrome* [sic] *will have to stand in front of Obama's death panel so his bureaucrats can decide, based on a subjective judgment of their level of productivity in society, whether they are worthy of healthcare. Such a system is downright evil.*[5]

After that, President Obama removed anything that smacked of a death committee from Obamacare. An extreme version of the death-panel accusation would be one that hinted at some kind of back-door euthanasia. There is a danger that, unless we bring these debates into the foreground, the very existence of secret committees making decisions about life and death will be used by enemies of the public sector to discredit it. During the COVID-19 crisis, the UK government, for a long time, refused to publish the membership of the now famous Scientific Advisory Group for Emergencies (SAGE) committee.

But what is this cowardice and fear that stops the sunlight of debate penetrating the administrative fog? How many times do we hear phrases such as "these are tough decisions", "there are limited resources" and "see that taxpayers money is well spent"? This is the voice of a patronising authority that claims it knows best, but at the same time exhibits a false confidence or even a deep insecurity. This insecurity surely comes not from the decisions themselves but from fear of the spotlight, whence in some far-off corner the sacrificed will rise up and ask, "Why me?". It is the voice of the vaccination-damaged child, the multiple sclerosis victim in pain denied the expensive drug, the old person denied intensive care facilities, the flood victim who sees the big expenditure going on compensation for airport runways and new roads, and the nurse or care worker in a pandemic without adequate personal protective equipment (PPE).

Another defence employed by the committee members and professorial advisors is the language of probability and risk. I feel doubly anxious about this because I am a professional statistician. The defence is as follows. Everyone has an equal chance of being the victim, so the system is fair. However, probability is no place to hide the sacrificed. The fact that the identities of the victims are not known before the event does not mean we should not call them victims after the event (apologies for the double negative). If there are victims, there is sacrifice. Wartime commanders know this. When they send soldiers into a dangerous operation, they estimate that some may die, even though they do not know in advance who they will be. The fact that they do not know does not – or should not – make the decision any easier for the commander or make the mission feel less dangerous for the front-line participants.

This essay is about the wild frontier of ethics, rather than the safe suburbs of utilitarianism, marginal utility, rational choice theory, etc. Reading ethics can be exhilarating in the same way that some might find reading religious texts exhilarating. But on the other hand, the material is often rich with theory rather than example, or uses only simplistic, artificial examples, so that some of the excitement is lost.

Taking scarcity and rationing as fixed constraints leads to the notion of "hard choices". We do not like the term, nor the fact that politicians try to hide behind it. These are often not hard choices in some preordained way, rather they are *forced* choices. The politicians set the financial parameters and then do the forcing. Sophie's choice (in the eponymous book) was the hardest anyone could have to make, but it was forced.[6]

This work is not a fully fledged treatise on risk and ethics, and that is why it is called an essay. In fact, it can be seen as a series of essays, with each on a somewhat different theme. It starts with QALYs, but also discusses industrial accidents and vaccinations, which are both issues close to the realities of public life. It will show that there is a very strong theme of utilitarianism running through these areas, but one that, as I have said, is partly hidden. There are important threads linking chapters, such as proportionality, rights and democracy. Hopefully, the essay provides an antidote to the raw "one life = one million pounds" approach of the cost-benefits advocates and their free-market-economist allies, and is able to lay down a path from William Blake's Spectre of simplistic rationality to the philosopher John Dewey's softer community-based democracy, and we shall find other allies along this path.

Many of the issues discussed in this essay are brought into sharp focus because of the climate emergency. Sacrifice is threatened, for example, to coastal and island communities because of sea-level rises. Duty of care issues, discussed in Chapter 6, are at the centre, and they will force governments to intervene, not necessarily because duty of care is suddenly to be enshrined in statute but because of the public clamour. The priority that we will recommend is *life itself*, which is one reason that a deeper narrative of individual events will be encouraged. Waiting till causation is proved using centuries of climate data is like using huge clinical trials in medicine to counter the worry about counterfactuals. This may not satisfy the vaccination victim waiting for compensation, or the property owner who has lost their house in an exceptional forest fire. The data and modelling are essential, of course, but the subjective views of the participants and experts are equally so. After all, the biggest factors are often man-made. This is not to challenge but to suggest an enlargement of the scientific method, as some experts are trying to do with what is called "singular causation": better explanations of individual events.

And now a personal narrative from me, the author. By one of those once-in-a-lifetime ironies, when theory and speculation suddenly meet reality, this essay was put to bed while my partner and I were in isolation from the COVID-19 pandemic. The shortage of ventilators, PPE and testing is, at this very moment of writing, *forcing* choices on doctors. Another shock, although this time somewhat gratifying, was that in the final week of proof reading we see Mark Carney, ex Governor of the Bank of England, giving his third Reith Lecture covering some of the ground of this essay, although in a more temperate manner.[7]

2.

NICE QALYs

In London, about a mile north of the River Thames in the north-west sector of the intersection of the Farringdon Road and Rosebury Avenue is the Mount Pleasant Post Office, which is a central post office of the UK. The area is informally called Mount Pleasant. The name is an ironic tribute to Londoners' humour in adversity. There is a large Black Death burial ground under the site, and it was also used as a refuse dump. A word that is very close in meaning to "pleasant" in the English language is "nice". NICE is the acronym for the UK National Institute for Health and Clinical Care Excellence ("Care" and "Health" were added in 2012).[8] The irony cannot have been lost on those who chose the name. NICE is a good example of one of the committees, mentioned previously, which has responsibility for life-and-death decisions.

Here is a short explanation of QALYs.[9] Suppose a patient has a serious illness. If she continues receiving the standard treatment, she will live for one year and her quality of life will be 0.4. Note that 0 denotes the worst quality of life and 1 means the best quality of life. If she receives a new drug, she will live for one year three months (1.25 years), with a quality of life of 0.6. The new treatment is compared with standard care in terms of the QALYs gained.

> Standard treatment: 1 (year's extra life) × 0.4 = 0.6 QALYs
> New treatment: 1.25 (1 year 3 months of extra life) × 0.6 = 0.75 QALYs
> New treatment leads to 0.75 − 0.4 = 0.35 additional QALYs.

Now suppose that the cost of the new drug, for the full course of treatment, is £10,000 compared to £3,000 for the standard treatment. The difference in treatment cost (£7,000) is divided by the QALYs gained (0.35) to calculate the cost per QALY. So the new treatment would cost £20,000 per QALY. The cost per QALY is the critical number, which may – if too big – lead NICE to ban the new drug. If the going rate declared by NICE is £30,000, our patient makes it.

At the risk of losing the reader early in this essay, let us try a little arithmetic. We need two quantities: time (T) and quality of life (Q). A basic QALY is the value $X = QT$, for a particular treatment applied to a particular patient. We should note that zero is a special value: $T = 0$ means no time lived, not even a nanosecond, so $Q = 0$ means you are dead. In either case, $X = 0$. We can standardise the cost per QALY as being the cost when $X = 1$. Then the cost for the particular treatment is $cX = cQT$, for some value (c), the cost per QALY. As mentioned, NICE imposes a cost-per-QALY threshold, which we shall call C (upper case). When the cost per QALY for a patient, c (lower case) (or the difference between the old and new treatment), is above the threshold, that is to say $c > C$, the treatment is banned from use in the National Health Service (NHS) (although NICE says publicly that "We must take into account other factors when developing our guidance."[10]).

An immediate flaw is that the pair of values Q and T depends on the patient, as well as the treatment. A patient for whom X = QT is large would have a personal cost per QALY that is less than someone with a small QT value. This is because X is a denominator in a ratio: c is the total cost divided by X.

This leads to a difficulty immediately. If an individual's cost per QALY (c) is high enough to be subject to a ban, then we may be discriminating between people with the same disease. But if it is a blanket ban applied to everyone with the same disease, then those who might benefit most are sacrificed.

We could develop this at great length, but we do not wish to sup too long with the logicians of health economics. There are already enough inequalities around – inequalities of birth, genetics and income – without discriminating against people because they happen to have a disease that is more expensive to treat, or, as already mentioned, they have the bad "luck" of having the disease more seriously.

The research and public documents are at pains to say that the QALY is based on sound principles. These amount to various types of primitive utility theory derived from economics. NICE covers itself by saying it "never uses QALYs as the sole determinant in their decisions".[11] One of the best known of these principles is willingness to pay (WTP).[12] The idea is based on preference. The researcher presents panels of subjects with hypothetical bundles of medical services, and asks each panel member to score or rank the bundles, or to say simply which out of two bundles they prefer. The sessions in which people are asked these questions are sometimes called "discrete choice experiments". The same methods are used in market research, to test products or potential products that have bundles of attributes; for example, prospective new car models. Designing such experiments is an interesting subject for statisticians, who can draw on 100 years of theories of experimental design. The bundles have attributes and dimensions, and by reverse engineering from people's choices, we can estimate the hypothetical weights that people attach to individual attributes. If the choices are described in terms of WTP, then these weights can be considered, so the argument goes, to represent the monetary value of these utilities. At its most sophisticated, this in an attempt to ascertain people's hidden utility functions or preference orderings. In that case, the final composite WTP figures express some kind of average of people's preferences. We shall see later that these methods are also used to put monetary values on human life in areas outside health economics, notably in health and safety.

Now we can move from the realm of medicine to see how *real* economists handle such things. They use something called a "social welfare function". This tries to combine the welfare of different groups into a portmanteau index, which can be used as a welfare function for the whole of society. Being very fond of having some quantity to maximise or minimise, the economists suggest that a welfare function can be used to guide policy in deciding how resources are allocated. [13]

Health is tied into this framework with a mathematical apparatus called a "health-related social welfare function". This could, for example, be the sum or average of all the individual QALYs in the population we are studying. But this leads to a quandary: does spending equitably mean spending so that everyone gets the same increase in health per unit of resource, or do we spend more on those whose health is worse? We can represent options such as this by using different mathematical formulae. Or, even neater, we can write down one big formula and let the parameter values in the formula do all the work. A useful tip in learning any new field – or, to be more precise, the equations of a new field – is to check out not only the main variables but what the other parameters mean – and their units! So in our equations or function, we should maybe have a special parameter called R (to stand for Rawls) so that when $R = 1$, we spend more (per QALY gain) on the most sick or if $R = 0$, award everyone the same gain. A sliding scale for equality. Why not?

With a small dose of mathematics, an introductory class in economics, and a computer to draw nice curves, this material is quite accessible. But the exercise gets a bit trickier when we ask another provocative question: who gets to choose the parameter values in the latest social welfare function? Is it you, esteemed reader; a panel; NICE; our local community health commissioners; the European Commission; the United Nations (UN); or Uncle Tom Cobley himself?

In the UK, there is a continuing obsession with panels. Ignoring any difficulty with the definition of the word "lay", it could be said that a panel is a group of lay people. They could be chosen at random, whatever that means, or appointed. We could put them in a room, with a cup of tea (very important in the UK), and ask them to choose some parameter values; e.g. the value of our newly coined Rawls constant, R. Or we could isolate them each at their own desk and ask them to choose values that we would combine to get an overall parameter estimate. The word "choice", which is still fashionable, makes it all sound very friendly and unthreatening. Seductive mathematical theories of choice discuss the possibility or impossibility of coming to a consensus under certain innocent axioms.

But there is something wrong in the way that we, the lays and the same Joe Publics who are allocated only a handful of positions on the official committees that make decisions about life and death, may be invited in – at a much lower level in the political hierarchy – to be research guinea pigs whose choices are inputs to some mathematical formula. The outputs of this formula are then passed to the appointed members of an ABCD committee that then chooses the Rawls number R, after a two-hour tutorial in the morning and a nice lunch. Apparently, we are good enough to score, but not good enough to decide.

In social science and medicine, some of the best studies are those that follow people over a long period. Cohort studies track people in a particular age group, studying the effects of social background, health, education and so on. In randomised clinical trials, people are followed for months and years afterwards, and sophisticated statistical methods are used to measure survival. It is often thought that results for cancer patients are likely to be better if they are admitted to a trial, because they will benefit from regular and detailed attention. Even for well-established, routine treatments, it is common to track patients for a number of years, via outpatient visits, and patients are advised to see their general practitioner (GP) if they have extra concerns. The generic term is "follow-up".

As is pointed out elsewhere in this essay, establishing causation in a complex treatment environment and combining that with demographic information about individuals is both important and difficult. One of the difficulties is the idea that you need counterfactuals to prove causation. The simplest way to solve this is with a control. There needs to be a basis for comparison to measure efficacy. However, in many situations in which we would like to establish causation, a pure control is not available in the sense that there is not some parallel universe with an exact clone of the subject albeit who does not get the drug under otherwise identical conditions.

Another key idea is that of intervention. If we have a smoothly running process and then intervene in a way that changes the process, we may be able to argue that intervention caused the change. The counterfactual is what would have happened had we not intervened. This is sometimes called a "before-and-after study". In some circumstances, it may be the best we can do. The calls for so-called "evidence-based policymaking" stem from the need to establish causation, and to avoid the decisions having the opposite effects to those intended. Far from being mysterious, it is the basis of much preventative action. If I don't go to the doctor, I will get (even) worse; if I don't spend money on my bicycle maintenance, then – like me – it may collapse when I least want it to. (Maybe I should dump it anyway and get an electric scooter?)

Now consider the banning of a drug as one would a medical intervention. This is a situation that needs counterfactuals, in the sense that we would like to know the effect of *not* banning it. Assume, for the sake of argument, that the efficacy of a drug in terms of QALYs is well known. This ought to be the case, because NICE says that its review process is very rigorous. Evidence of follow-ups for the patients *denied* treatment is harder to find. We are not here to suggest that the denial should somehow be considered as an actual trial, in the sense of a rigorous experiment to establish the efficacy of the treatment. To repeat, the NICE review should already have established causation. But society does deserve to know how many people were affected by the denial, and by how much. If the arithmetic of QALYs was used to make the drug-denial decision, then we deserve to know the full effect of that decision.

Suppose you were born into a poor family, your parents are out of work, and you have a genetic disposition to catch disease Z. Now suppose that, on top of one or more of these inequalities, you have another one: Z is expensive to treat. It seems this is no more or less than an additional structural inequality. Of course, those in favour of the more utilitarian approaches to health economics can always counter this by discussing the cost of the very, very expensive drug that can only extend life by a few months. Yes, we can sit down and discuss such cases, but let us have the other structural inequalities on the agenda too. While we are about it, we really ought to discuss, with the same rigour and commitment, the tax-avoidance schemes of the rich. I could certainly suggest some interventions in that regard.

Throughout this book, we will find simple statements that, hopefully, when taken together, serve to frame the idea of sacrifice. A rough definition is that it exists when decisions that disadvantage individuals are driven by some kind of rationing, scarcity or political necessity, but where, at the same time, there is an absence of any broader discussion of social justice. And this is not just some cry for old-fashioned values; there is a huge body of evidence demonstrating that social inequalities lead to health inequalities. On health grounds alone, we should take a wider perspective.

Of course, NICE and similar bodies are aware of some of these issues. NICE's Technological Appraisal Guidance leads to mandatory recommendations. But most detailed decisions are left to Clinical Commissioning Groups (CCGs), which operate within finite local budgets that are imposed from the centre. As a kind of acknowledgement of this outsourcing of risk and ethics, there is what is termed a "procedural right" (sometimes qualified as "procedural fairness"), which lies alongside the decision, such as the right to deny any expensive treatments for patients. The documents say there should be a rational procedure by which the decision is made and that the patient should be told about.[14]

In the last chapter of this book, we shall promote the importance of community. Indeed, the balance between central and local decision-making is crucial. The difficulty at the moment is that the documents related to the procedural rights cling to the same subservience to a utilitarian point of view that operates at the centre. It is historically of interest that the concept of rationality, which is a hallmark of "rational choice theory" and "rational expectation", the archetypal engine of free-market economics, has crept to the front line of resource allocation: Sorry we are killing you by withdrawing your drug, but just look at how rational we are being.

There is a single word appearing in the documents issued to CCGs that summarises the hidden trade-offs being recommended at the local level, based on principles and budgets laid down at the national level. The word is "disinvestment".[15] This revolting euphemism means removing a particular treatment, typically on cost grounds. Never was there a more Orwellian term in health. The documents say "disinvestments should be considered along with investments". Imagine being told, under your procedural rights, that your particular area of illness has been disinvested. Sorry, children, your grandmother was disinvested.

The fundamental issue of whether those who make the decisions actually have the right to choose who lives and who dies, is rarely discussed. But ethical training seems to be creeping up the agenda for members of CCGs.[16]

What happened to the founding ideals of the NHS? There is a simple answer. There was a new constitution in 2007, which had a brand new Principle 1(6): "The NHS is committed to providing best value for taxpayers' money and the most effective, fair and sustainable use of finite resources."[17] It is time to recall Aneurin "Nye" Bevan, the father of the NHS, in full flow:

> *The Chancellor of the Exchequer in this year's Budget proposes to reduce the Health expenditure by £13 million – only £13 million out of £4,000 million… If he finds it necessary to*

mutilate, or begin to mutilate, the Health Services for £13 million out of £4,000 million, what will he do next year? Or are you next year going to take your stand on the upper denture? The lower half apparently does not matter, but the top half is sacrosanct. Is that right?... The Chancellor of the Exchequer is putting a financial ceiling on the Health Service. With rising prices the Health Service is squeezed between that artificial figure and rising prices. What is to be squeezed out next year? Is it the upper half? When that has been squeezed out and the same principle holds good, what do you squeeze out the year after? Prescriptions? Hospital charges? Where do you stop? [18]

The term "taxpayer" is often used from a right-wing perspective, but masquerading as a neutral term that conveys some kind of financial accountability. It may be no coincidence that, in the UK, the introduction of the word into the NHS constitution coincided with the rise of the Taxpayers' Alliance, a right-wing organisation started by a friend of Margaret Thatcher.[19] The taxpayer is that one-dimensional person who is always wanting a smaller state and always queuing up to shoot arrows into the public sector. It is one thing to say, very sensibly, that the public sector should seek value for money in its operations and continually improve its internal efficiency, but the taxpayer is a grotesque representation of the citizen as a cardboard-cut-out ranter. I have a vision of the same taxpayer waiting in pain to be seen in a cash-starved accident-and-emergency unit.

Taxpayers do not appear, thankfully, in the statutes of NICE, but it did not take long to find them on NICE's webpages: "Applying NICE's evidence-based model to public policymaking could help to save billions of pounds of taxpayers' money by helping doctors, head teachers, police chiefs and many others make smarter decisions based on what works and what doesn't."[20] One can also find them lurking in speeches of the NICE directorate.

A small digression. Art, literature and poetry are often best when they provide a vehicle for us to use our own imaginations. Drama on radio, which I happen to love, has this effect: all the visualisation is done internally by the listener. Poetry stimulates our emotions, and we often do not know why. Maybe it's because it comes in concentrated packets? Just one or two lines can provide an emotional trigger; music the same. Let us quote one of the great poets, Samuel Taylor Coleridge:

> *The primary IMAGINATION I hold to be the living Power and prime Agent of all human Perception, and as a repetition in the finite mind of the eternal act of creation in the infinite I AM. The secondary Imagination I consider as an echo of the former, co-existing with the conscious will, yet still as identical with the primary in the kind of its agency, and differing only in degree, and in the mode of operation. It dissolves, diffuses, dissipates, in order to recreate; or where this process is rendered impossible, yet still at all events it struggles to idealize and unify. It is essentially vital, even as all objects (as objects) are essentially fixed and dead.*[21]

There are many objections to the use of economics in matters of life and death, and I will address them throughout this essay. However, the biggest problem with the utilitarian approach is that it fails to tell the story of our lives, which is a failure of imagination. If cash resources are limited and some group is favoured over another, and if a person in the unfavoured group suffers or dies as a consequence, then that person has, to my mind, been sacrificed. But in the formulae, the equations, the statistics from the panel studies, and the long and learned reports, the voices of the sacrificed are seldom heard. It is as if they are on another hill – the "Mount of Externalities" – far away, out of sight and out of mind. If asked to run their own personal-choice experiment they would surely say, "No, I do not want to die; that is not my *choice*."

Society is a rich collection of individuals, and no naïve mathematical formula can incorporate all their needs and desires. People go to hospital, and they are treated as well as the hospital is able. A hospital is no place for sacrifice. There should not have to be a choice between saving one patient and saving another. That happens in warfare and famines when they run out of medical supplies or food. When there is a peacetime emergency, such as a train crash or a bombing atrocity, they call in extra doctors and resources. They do not, or should not, make sacrificial choices. They would not say, "Sorry, this looks like a rather expensive event, so we can only let you have two ambulances." However, while the valiant hospital staff try to treat people as people and value each the same – young and old, male and female, black and white – their masters are cooking up formulae (the fashionable word is "algorithms") that build in the sacrifice of one group for another, and set one group against another, thereby destroying the whole notion of the public good.

We need to be reminded of Article 2 of the European Convention on Human Rights: "Everyone's right to life shall be protected by law."[22] It is essentially illegal to kill one person to save the life of another. Compare this with one of the ugliest methodologies in health economics namely the person trade-off (PTO).[23] The name says it all. This is an extreme type of choice experiment in which a bundle of, say, ten patients who would benefit from a life-saving treatment is to be compared with another bundle of N other patients who would benefit from a different treatment. Respondents are asked to play

God by saying at what value of N would you be indifferent to the variations between the two groups. I side with those who refused to participate in such a study.

Even when people play God, a certain shyness can creep in. For the NICE committee where voting is anonymous, there were rumours at one time that members are asked to put their vote onto a piece of yellow paper, which they then fold and hand to the chair. The Spanish Inquisition had better rules:

> *Each voter shall be at liberty to make any observation which he thinks proper in giving his vote, without being interrupted or prevented. If the inquisitors give different votes, they shall explain their motives, to prove that there is nothing to arbitrate in their conduct. The recorder shall write each opinion in the register prepared for the purpose, and shall afterwards join it to the trial to give testimony to it.*[24]

3.

Forced choices and the rise of proportionality

Placing a value on human life is an old story, and one not confined to the cogwheels of health economics. In 1949, the wife of a miner who had been killed by the collapse of the supporting structure of a coalmine roadway sued the National Coal Board. The miner's name was Edwards and the case is often referred to as "Edwards v National Coal Board". Mrs Edwards lost the case, and the judgement deeply influenced the history of health and safety in the UK, right up to the present day. The Court of Appeal changed the term "physically possible" in the first judgement to "reasonably practicable":

> 'Reasonably practicable' is a narrower term than 'physically possible' and implies that a computation must be made... in which the quantum of risk is placed in one scale and the sacrifice involved in the measures necessary for averting the risk (whether in time, trouble or money) is placed in the other and that, if it be shown that there is a great disproportion between them – the risk being insignificant in relation to the sacrifice –

the person upon whom the obligation is imposed discharges the
onus which is upon him.[25]

The ruling became embodied into safety methodology as "so far as is reasonably practical" (SFAIRP), and the sister term used in what is today termed "risk analysis" is "as low as is reasonably practicable" (ALARP). Both terms appear in the UK Health and Safety Act, 1974: "It shall be the duty of every employer to ensure, so far as is reasonably practicable, the health, safety and welfare at work of all his employees."[26] Not much has changed since Edwards v National Coal Board.

The legal attractiveness of these ideas, particularly the term "reasonably practicable", is that it sets up a principle, or a benchmark, by which to judge individual cases. The principles have also been reinforced by a lot of case law. The advantage for employers is that they know broadly where they stand in their duty to protect their workers. Conversely, it makes it much harder for employees to sue, because they have to establish negligence or grossly disproportionate action. Thus "proportionate" and "proportionality" are now terms by which many judgements are made in what amounts to a perverse kind of legal cost-benefit analysis (CBA).

The European Commission has challenged the use of SFAIRP in the UK, claiming that it is against one of its directives, but it lost the case on 18 January 2007. The ruling was overruled by the European Court of Justice. In an excruciating double negative it said:

The Commission has not established to the requisite legal
standard that, in qualifying the duty of employers to ensure the
safety and health of workers in every aspect related to work by
limiting the duty to what is reasonably practicable, the United

*Kingdom has failed its obligation under Article 5(1) and (4) of
the Directive 89/391.*[27]

Since then there have been a number of reports in the
UK reflecting the steady lobbying of industry against the
"bureaucratic burdens" of health and safety, under the wider
umbrella of doing away with red tape. The most notorious of
these was the European Union's (EU's) High Level Working
Group on Administrative Burdens, chaired by the controversial
Bavarian right-winger Dr Edward Stoiber.[28] The group came up
with radical proposals to slash health and safety regulations,
particularly for small and medium-sized enterprises (SMEs).
Part of the reason back then for the radical approach appears
to have been the need to appease a UK government keen to cut
back on red tape coming from the EU. Four members of the
group put in a minority report and the general secretary of the
UK Trades Union Congress (TUC) stated:

*It is no wonder that Stoiber failed to get the support of
the whole group when its proposals were published. It
threatened to put workers and consumers at risk by scrapping
some employment rights, health and safety duties and
environmental protection.*[29]

We should be very concerned with definitions of SFAIRP,
ALARP and CBA and the day-to-day politics of health and
safety, because there is a profound theme playing, one which, if
not exactly hidden, is at least coyly absent from the front pages;
for example, the introductory webpages of the UK Health and
Safety Executive (HSE). The superstructure housing these rules
is built on the *cash value of a human life*. This provides a direct
link to QALYs. The figures can be found by digging into the use

of WTP methodology by the HSE; the latest current value for what HSE call "human cost" is £1,296,000.[30]

Let us put it as simply as we can. In a dubious logical twist, the value of a human life is equated to the value of preventing an accident that would end a human life. The irony is that health and safety is an example of an area that has hijacked the idea of sacrifice, ever since the original Edwards v the National Coal Board judgement. It means, in official terms, the amount a company should sacrifice to avoid a worker fatality. At least it could have the decency to be more balanced or more honest. It could at a minimum be what the company, which legally means the shareholders, should sacrifice to avoid the sacrifice of a worker.

The use of the word "sacrifice" with this inverted meaning has a long history. The principle of equal sacrifice – which, sadly, goes back at least to John Stuart Mill – says that, in some sense, there should be equity in taxation. This is variously taken to be equal amounts, as in a poll tax, or equal proportions. Mathematical elaborations are based on utility theory, which are versions of the idea that if you have more money, you don't mind (proportionally to your income) losing so much. But the word "sacrifice" used in technical phrases such as "the fiscal sacrifice of the rich" is, to my mind, inappropriate and offensive. There is a thesis to be written about the concepts of generosity and sacrifice of large charities built with corporate profits. Should we apply the word "sacrifice" to the Melinda and Bill Gates Foundation?

As we have hinted, it seems that much of the progressive approach to health and safety in Europe has been deliberately thwarted by the anti-red-tape campaign. Meanwhile, the health and safety stalwarts trudge on, collecting and publishing data, having conferences, and supporting journals. I go to such conferences. Safety and reliability is one of the great success stories of applied statistics. Thank goodness, given the huge risks from nuclear accidents and the like. But the split between the anti-red-tape brigade and the safety black belts is a tragedy. The first group wants to hide behind ALARP and the second wants to promote the safety culture, when – to repeat – expenditure on health and safety is called a "sacrifice" for the company while workers are actually being physically sacrificed. The split is between political ideology (small state-ism and the free market) and duty of care. It does not take long to discover where this contrast is most evident. Immigrant labour in the construction industry has the highest fatality rate in many countries. This is like some kind of ghastly reminder of nineteenth-century UK. I feel like some ultra-left-wing propagandist as I write the following: globalisation unfettered by regulation leads to a mobility of labour by which immigrants are supplied to die on building sites. But it is true.

There is a single word that separates the two philosophies: *acceptance*. If we start by saying no injury or death is acceptable, then we have defined the safety culture. Death on a building site is unacceptable, a single vaccine-damaged child is unacceptable, and no death from the denial of a drug is acceptable. A sacrifice may happen, and we may not have the science to stop it, but it is never acceptable. Acceptance implies some kind of trade-off. Beware the term "trade-off" in contributions to ethical debates such as "there must be a trade-off". Must? Who says so?

In fact, history is on the side of zero acceptance. Every major accident – from Three Mile Island to Piper Alpha, and from Exxon Valdez to Hurricane Katrina – has led to improved safety. Ralph Nader, in his book *Unsafe at Any Speed*, changed the automobile industry forever: "over half a century the automobile has brought death, injury, and the most inestimable sorrow and deprivation to millions of people".[31] It has become illegal to produce vehicles that are intrinsically unsafe.

The safety culture should and does permeate product design. We cannot have driverless vehicles pottering around our cities without the best design standards, supported by regulation. One accident is one too many. We cannot have exploding mobile phones. When we think about driverless cars or the fashionable but apparently rather dangerous electric scooters, we imagine a bright, new "smart city" in which we move around in a society of equals – drivers, driverless, pedestrians, cyclists and public transport passengers – not a competitive race track. In such an environment, death is not acceptable. In fact, it is not acceptable in Formula 1 racing, if it ever was, even though some ghoulish spectators may like to see a crash. However, there seems to be an alien moral world where matters are engineered politically to create a level of acceptability; a world in which the roof of a coal mine or scaffolding on a building site can collapse, and we are told that there is an acceptable level of proportionality related to expenditure on safety. There is no acceptable level if you are the family of a dead worker.

SMEs are agreed to be the fountains of enterprise and innovation. We are proud of our Silicon Valleys, Silicon Glens and Silicon Roundabouts, and our universities boast about their science parks with their SME incubation pods. These should not be sweatshops with light-touch regulation on health and safety. In fact, we can argue the reverse, simply on pragmatic grounds. A small start-up company that ignores safety may grow into a big company that ignores safety, just as a small firm that ignores quality or gathers personal data illegally may grow into a big firm that does the same. Eventually, they may lose market share and go bankrupt. This should all be obvious, but the various documents issued by the UK government try to square the circle.

They pay lip service to the safety culture while being very careful to remind industry of the financial limits of its responsibility.

My own father spent much of his career in mine safety. I was an attentive child in a family with an interest in scientific matters. One perennial topic was fire: fire in tunnels, fire in chimneys and fire in shafts. So, when the horrific Grenfell Tower fire took hold, all of it on television, I knew in some kind of instinctive way that the cladding was burning, accelerated by a chimney effect. I guessed also that there must have been a gross failure in rules and regulations. In a less than scholarly way, I tweeted old newspaper headlines from before the fire such as Prime Minister Cameron's "I shall destroy the safety culture".[32] I included articles about cutbacks in safety regulations, such as the slashing of the HSE's budget and the abolition of road-safety targets (in England). Many reporters were delving into the same seam of material, which included similar fires around the world that could also be attributed to the wrong cladding.

In a compulsive way I tracked down the infamous BR 135 document promoted by the Building Research Establishment (BRE), which permitted the use of so-called "desktop reports" that allowed the use of previous information to testify to the safety of the cladding with the riders – which proved correct – that there had often been no adequate fire testing to base such reports on, or where it was adequate, it was ignored. In fact, the serious testing was done *after* the Grenfell Tower fire. I tracked the cosy relationship between the HSE, the BRE and building companies. I noted how the webpages of organisations had been taken down while they were writing their "statements on Grenfell" and how others, particularly architects and consultants, trotted out holier-than-thou we-told-you-so statements. It did and still does look like a case of "regulatory capture". Yes, the relationships were too cosy, with too many company employees on safety bodies and too much of the anti-red-tape ethos surviving from around 2010. I collected what I had been learning and gave some evidence to one of the inquiries.

It will be clear by now that much, if not all, of this book is about difficult decisions. In the ethics literature, the phrase "hard choices" is used. Although I have probably offended a few professions, such as politicians and economists, I hope that the conclusions are uncontroversial and also reasonably coherent. I have rejected the vision of libertarianism espoused by writers such as Nozick, and I want to stay closer the Rawlsian vision.

It may be helpful to have a metaphor in mind. This can be topographical, or mathematical if we prefer. Topographically, we can think of the hard choices as peaks in some ethical landscape, and – to push the metaphor – suppose the peaks are sharp. In an as-yet-undeveloped total mathematical theory of ethics (God forbid), we can suppose that these peaks are like singularities. Ironically, this is almost too strong a metaphor because, in mathematics, a singularity is sometimes a site (in some mathematical space) where a quantity goes to infinity. Just like peaks can be climbed, singularities can be "resolved" in mathematics. Since we are against sacrifice, if every peak represents a potential sacrifice, then, above all, *we need to try to remove them*. We want a fairer society, and this means a softer ethical landscape. It is worth noting that there is scholarly work discussing whether the value of a human life should indeed be labelled as infinite. That may be the starting point for an ambitious student who might want to be first with the creation of a theory of "ethics with singularities". Good luck!

It really should not be the case that, in the UK, choices have to be made as to who gets the intensive care unit. There should be sufficient units at the right location or close by. It really should not be the case that the underfunding, or poor design, of cycle lanes in London has led to deaths, while billions of pounds are spent on the (not yet finished) Crossrail project. One should not have to make these choices. It should not be the case that, in an epidemic, there are not enough antiviral drugs to go round. It should not be the case that a vaccine with known side effects continues to be used without a search for a safer vaccine and hefty compensation for the victims of the side effects.

So what about this landscape of hard choices? Can we give ourselves a few instruments to survey it? We have seen several presented by NICE and by the HSE: QALY, WTP, WTA (willingness to accept), ALARP and SFAIRP. We have also seen that, in the case of life and death, the value of a human life underpins much of the official thinking.

Is it possible, without getting too technical, to find out why it is – at least to this author – a distasteful business that equates life with money? There is a large literature on one particular aspect of the conundrum, which is the gap between WTP and WTA. Recall that WTP is the willingness to pay for some good, and WTA covers the compensation for giving something up. We can see easily that the relationship depends on whether, in the case of WTP, you feel you deserve it in the first place. It is sometimes called your "property rights". The example given often is if you bought your property with an expectation of an unpolluted lake next to it, you may be reluctant to pay for cleaning the lake. For WTA, the converse applies: if someone wants to pollute the lake, they had better pay big compensation. Many studies show that WTA is usually much larger than WTP, and many different explanations have been given. Perhaps the most convincing is what is called the "endowment effect": giving something up is more painful than the positive expectation of owning something new.[33]

But in the literature, there is reluctance to talk about life and death, despite the rush to put a monetary value on life. Part of this avoidance is a special technique used at the foundation of economics, which is to look at the *marginal* values: studying how a small change in expenditure would pay for a small change in, say, life expectancy or the curing of a disease. The hope is that, by integrating all these small effects, one can construct some kind of global quantification. For the mathematically minded, give me the differential equation and I will give you the integral. We also need boundary conditions; we can only build a good simulation of real ripples from a stone dropped into a real pond if we know the pond's shape, size and depth, and even the interface with the air.

When the endowment is life, we are on the real and mathematical boundary. For one thing, all the smoothness that happens with the mathematics of the differential calculus breaks down. But there is a much more difficult problem, one at the heart of any theory of hard choices, and that is "incommensurability". Although there are various definitions, we can take one of the most straightforward: A is preferred to B on one measurement scale, but B is preferred to A on another. We could refine this. Very much related is incomparability: A and B are so different in their essence that we just cannot compare them on any scale. Try to compare the colour (A) of a flower with its scent (B).[34]

At the heart of this essay is the incommensurability between the values placed on important possessions by society and those placed by the individual, particularly for life itself. Nearly every expert points out that, in terms of compensation for one's own life or that of a close family member, there is no limit to what one might pay. We have a singularity. We could take a very strong view that life and money are incommensurate, but that is not our main point right now. It is evident that the value is in the eye of the beholder. Asked what someone would pay for their own survival or for that of a family member, the answer is "everything I have". Some writers discuss asking someone on their deathbed how much they would be willing to pay to live. To economists, this puts an upper bound on the WTP. In fact, crowdfunding operations reaching out to family, friends, plus sympathetic strangers, can today raise thousands of pounds to fund a special operation or a special drug to save a person's life. In this case, the very notion of society becomes fragmented.

The value that NICE, the HSE and the Ministry of Transport put on life does not bear any relation to what you and I might put on *our* lives. A stark example that we have already discussed is compensation for work-based death. First, the requirements to be fulfilled by companies are neatly enclosed in SFAIRP, etc., then the compensation for accidents in the UK is gradually incorporated into standard compensation schemes, such as widow's benefits. The only hope to get decent compensation is to sue. This is clear from the army of legal practices offering to help. This alone is indicative of a huge gap between what "society" thinks compensation should be and what the victim's family thinks the rightful compensation should be. It is even possible to give a rough estimate.

There seems to me to be a deep contradiction in the whole approach. On the one hand, the economist can develop interesting theories based on the rational individual, but as soon as there are hard choices to be made, these theories lead to obvious incommensurate features, and there is a tendency to fall back on some societal measure such as WTP. This massive leap is, of course, very convenient for policymakers, and it may even be acceptable to the individual on a smaller and local scale, in the arena of the marginal effects, but not on the large scale. There is some recognition of the gap between the WTP and WTA, and the concept of the public good. There is evidence that estimates of WTP are not realistic when the item is a public good. One argument says that, in effect, the public good is not tangible enough, compared to a good that benefits people directly. Some writers then go on to argue that WTP should therefore not be used at all for public-expenditure decisions.

In the equation "one human life = £1,296,000", we should think clearly about the equals sign. It is simply not legitimate that the equals signs that do such great service in mathematics and science should be dropped over human affairs, despite being primed with the modern theories of choice and game theory, and behind a smoke screen of proportionality.

Incommensurability, in its strong sense, is a refusal to compare entities. Chalk seems incommensurate with cheese. With ingenuity, we can cook up metrics on which they can be compared. Cheese is probably a better present to give as a dinner guest, although a beautiful pack of drawing chalk has originality in its favour. Scales on which there is some basis for comparison are sometimes called "covering scales" or metrics. It seems to me that coming up with covering scales often seems contrived. There must be a clear distinction between some kind of objective or universal covering values and the subjective values. It would be better to highlight metrics on which we could agree and then investigate the extent of the incommensurability of those.

Ironically, risk management at its less monetary end – that is, away from mathematical finance and the like – has actually identified several other such types of risk, including reputational risk and risks related to business ethics and customer satisfaction. Medicine also has incommensurate non-monetary risks in the definitions of "quality of life", such as pain and disability, despite the attempts to force them into a single covering metric: the QALY. This is, of course, before the rush to translate the risks into cost to the NHS and the taxpayer, and to shareholders in the case of the private sector. When all attempts at finding covering values fail, then we may use the term "incomparable", meaning no basis for comparison.

But there *are* universal metrics. One such is the total ban on torture. There are no mitigating circumstances that a government may put forward to justify or excuse torture. There are also two universal rules that can be used as objective benchmarks.

> Rule 1. It is not permissible to take a human life to save another human life, at least in peacetime.

> Rule 2. The Golden Rule: do not do to others what you would not want done to yourself.

Much of health economics breaks both rules. To steal from our introduction: do not deprive someone else's grandmother of intensive care if you would not wish your own grandmother to be so deprived.

In many cases, there is a lack of balance between the players. These are not convenient two-person, zero-sum games, lotteries with known odds, or textbook battles between capital and labour or customers versus company. In many of the cases, one side is an individual and their family, and the other is a state or a large organisation. Coming before the European Court of Justice, we find cases of individuals set against not even a state but the policy of the state in a particular area, be it health and safety, immigration, or the voting rights of prisoners. Moreover, the policy may not be so clearly stated, or it may be filtered through committees, regulations and case law. This makes the use of the equals sign in our ethical equations even more problematical.

The aforementioned Rule 1 should not only be embedded in our culture, but it exposes a deep chasm between the rights of the individual and a limited idea of the public good. This mistake, which is what Rawls seeks to solve, is the separation of the public good from the individual. Put bluntly, *it cannot be part of the public good to sacrifice an individual for the public good.* It is no good wielding "the greatest good for the greatest number", so the solution – perhaps the only solution – is to extend the notion of public good (wherever it is not already extended) into the craggy peaks of ethics. And the analogy is not bad. We send lifeboats and helicopters to those in peril on the sea. We send out rescue missions to find lost explorers, climbers and cavers. Firemen crawl through burning buildings. No one could argue that all that is not in the public good.[35]

There are many critiques of utilitarianism, and many pitfalls in related areas of ethics. A profound argument from Alistaire Macintyre is that ethics lost its way sometime during the Enlightenment, and that mechanistic ideas contained within the very successful application of the scientific method were responsible. We can select various versions of utilitarianism stemming from Jeremy Bentham and John Stuart Mill's father, James Mill, and add a dose of mathematical economics based on the primitive use of utility. We then stir in some human rights to act as a sweetener. The tension between rights and utilitarian ideas is nowhere more evident that with John Stuart Mill. There have been attempts to qualify or constrain utilitarianism by rules. We see such ideas throughout optimisation in economics: keep the objective function the same, but change the constraints. Maximise profit subject to regulatory constraints, safety constraints, etc. Therefore, it is argued, we can maximise the overall good (greatest happiness) subject to everyone receiving what is their right.

But please be suspicious when the outcome you are interested in is demoted to being expressed via a constraint, which is what rights-based utilitarianism (as just described) gives us. Our qualms can arise in practical examples. An oil or gas company may declare it wishes to make the biggest profit it can, subject to low carbon targets; sell diesel cars subject to constraints on emissions; and celebrate when it has been able to maximise the engine efficiency and get the emissions marginally just below the limits. Think of the frustration of the engineer when forced to put in new emission constraints late in the day; optimisation with extra constraints is such a bore.

As time goes by, the constraints may get tighter. No more the joy of wriggling young toes in the X-ray machine in the shoe shop. The so-called "safe limits for the radiation exposure of workers" has decreased slowly, despite opposition from the nuclear industry, but under a strangely familiar term: as low as is reasonably achievable (ALARA). The interest in the medical effects of particle size has dropped through PM10 to PM2.5, with some researchers claiming that there should be no lower limit: no particles at all is best.[36]

A main argument for rights is to protect the individual from extreme versions of sacrifice for the public good in cases where the individual's needs are swamped by the needs of the rest of society or used in a David-and-Goliath situation. However, to some degree, casting this as an incommensurability problem is playing into the hands of the utilitarians. To say that there is no covering metric hints that if there were a covering metric, everything would be fine, we could toss a coin, or we could leave it to the judge's intuition. On the other hand, a commitment to rights or rules extends the moral range. Thus, another rule is this:

Rule 3. Equality: equal treatment.

After the seminal work of Atkinson and Piketty,[37] equality is rising up the political agenda. We can say that sacrifice is an extreme version of inequality, but it may need another book to develop that idea further. The idea of equality is embedded in definitions of the social contract and the fact that, unless we cling to it, great economic and political forces will erode it. Globalisation may have decreased economic inequality – this case is often made for China – but the case is not clear for "moral equality": dignity, respect, social justice, natural rights, human worth and so on. There are principles for the equal distribution of public resources, and the idea that equality should only be about that distribution. Equality may be a resource issue, but one matter seems clear to me: without massive qualification, utilitarianism has not made much room for equality. It is not much comfort to the sacrificed that they were part of a good average.

A favourite word of law and regulations makers is "risk", and in other areas, "proportionality". The latter implies that, in taking some action or making a judgement, the decision-maker should act in a proportionate way. Typically, it is used when there is some kind of imbalance in the power relationship: David-and-Goliath cases. It is used to underpin the amount of punishment for a crime, as in the old question: does the punishment fit the crime? It has been championed by the European Court of Human Rights as a way of balancing the rights of the individual with the national policies of individual states in areas such as immigration and redundancy. It is well captured in the following ruling:

> *An interference with a basic right in the treaty is warranted only if (1) it pursues a legitimate objective compatible with the Treaty and is justified by (2) overriding reasons of public interest*

[justifiable means]; if this is the case, it must be (3) suitable for securing the attainment of the objective which it pursues and (4) not go beyond what is necessary in order to attain it.[38]

Proportionality, from a mathematical point of view, means there are two scales and that the value chosen on one scale is proportional to the value on the other scale. It is easier when the same units are used on the two scales. Thus, if there are two people and tax is proportional to income, then they each pay the same proportion of their income in tax. It is harder when there are two different units, such as when property tax was (roughly) proportional to the area of windows in a building. But these are easy cases. Proportionality in the legal/ethical arena often says that two different types of entity have to be proportionate: thus the punishment for stealing a lamb should be proportionate to the crime. Maybe someone who steals a lamb should be denied the possibility of eating lamb for a number of years. This sentiment prevails in community service as an alternative to prison. A crime may be against a victim in a community, and the sentence is to put something back into the community.

However, in general, the concept of proportionality is fraught with problems. It seems to imply some kind of background method of comparing non-comparable things. Let's look at the scent and colour of our flowers again. We could set up a sensory-testing experiment to establish some kind of order of preference, but even if we were able to do this, there would be a region in the middle where we could not honestly choose between flowers. In many of the cases at issue, we have individual rights up against some kind of common good. One of the critiques is that the measurement is one-sided. While it may be quite easy to measure the effects on the individual of some court verdict, the common good is typically much harder to pin down.

It is of considerable interest that the idea of proportionality began in relation to warfare, given our opening paragraph suggesting that rules applying in warfare are inappropriate in peacetime. Modern proportionality has emerged steadily as a general principle of law. The legal principle first articulated in the law of nations (the synonym is *jus gentium*; i.e. public international law) was increasingly applied in cases of self-defence, not only of states but also of the person, and then in national criminal and administrative law. The right to self-defence must be exercised no more than is proportional to the threat. Punishments should be proportional to crimes; the administration must not act excessively.

Let us try to ground these ideas more accurately in ethical theory. Rawls sets up a thought experiment to find the principles of justice and to design institutions that would administer them. We can understand this by analogy. There is a quaint and somewhat pompous custom in the UK in that the members of a committee or commissions who make important decisions should "leave their hats outside the room". This is an acknowledgement that members may have outside interests that could affect their judgement. In a thought experiment, Rawls imagines that citizens are having to construct a society in which they do not yet know their own personal position. Since they may find themselves disadvantaged personally, the natural inclination should be to use "maximin"; that is, to maximise the position of the worst off. This is a version of social-contract theory with a Kantian flavour, since it describes how to construct a social contract while claiming to be rights based. But it can also be thought of as a version of utilitarianism that operates a new kind of utility based on maximin, rather than average welfare.

Let us test, for the sake of argument, the idea that there is a coherent and rational theory of ethics somewhere in this nexus of ideas. We can play the game of suggesting questions to test such a theory. Here are some: (i) Would you want to be sacrificed for the public good? (ii) Would you want to be sacrificed for the public good, without compensation? (iii) If you were sacrificed for the public good with compensation, how much do you think compensation should be?

Or we can craft a Kantian-style question: can it be a universal rule that an individual is sacrificed for the public good? We strengthen that question to this: can it be a universal rule that anyone has the possibility of being sacrificed for the public good? And, finally, this may become the following: is it part of the definition of the public good to have a universal rule that anyone has the possibility of being sacrificed for the public good? This is approaching nonsense, and it shows that combining universality with sacrifice is impossible.

It is of interest that a French law (see Chapter 5) appeals to the principle of equality, which is fundamental to the French constitution, to allow no-fault compensation for the adverse effects of administrative action, if the actions themselves are said to be in the public good. We are made to think that the cry of not me, not my grandmother or not my child is not a selfish cry but a demand for equality. We often read of medical or administrative mistakes where the family concerned has not asked for compensation, but simply demands that the responsible institutions act together so that the event does not happen again. This is surely because the event has deviated from a normal situation – a situation of stability and equality.

To some extent, we have put the cart before the horse in that we have been discussing the public good partly in terms of compensation for victims of government action. This was deliberate. If we start with definitions of public good, we may find that the term has been hijacked by the free-market economist as the sort of stuff that arises out of market failure, much in the same way that externalities are a kind of second-class citizen. It is also said that all this "public good" stuff is better undertaken by the private sector. We shall see later that the brutal free-market economics of the nineteenth century had a few dedicated critics back then. It took a long time until some kind of antidote appeared in various kinds of social democracy.

Vaccination is on a long list of public goods that are deemed by politicians and the public at large to be needed for overall public wellbeing, which also includes health and safety, food safety, environmental protection, education, law and order, and democratic institutions. As J. K. Galbraith states:

> *They are things that do not lend themselves to production, purchase and sale. They must be provided for by everyone if they are to be provided for anyone and they must be paid for collectively or they cannot be had at all.*[39]

There are many goods and services giving social and economic benefits so great that it is a no-brainer that they should be provided by the state. Typically, these form a natural monopoly and should only be carried out by private sector institutions if the regulations are strong enough to prevent exploitation. A very interesting class of services comes from networks: road networks, rail networks, water networks, energy networks (including district heating) and communication networks. Even though, for example, one can allow third-party access to have companies competing for customers, there is essentially only one national electricity network in the UK: the National Grid. It is surely only ideology that keeps the National Grid as a private company; this is the same for water.

There is tension between the right to life in Article 3 of the UN Universal Declaration of Human Rights,[40] which states that "Everyone has the right to life...", and Article 29's "Everyone has duties to the community...". Rights form one of the supporting bookends of a shelf of systems, at the other end of which is complete self-sacrifice for the greater good of society. Resolving the tension helps to define the social contract and democracy itself.

The trouble starts when the state commandeers the idea of society and, in extreme cases, tries to define itself by doing that. The subtle balance between thinking of one's own interests and those of the community – which might be achieved by a careful, democratic deliberation – becomes a fight between citizens trying to defend their rights and a state using a public-good argument to carry out a macro policy of some kind: e.g. bulldozing 5,000 houses and a number of ancient woodlands to make way for the new High Speed 2 (HS2) train services from London to Birmingham.

The starting premise of this essay is that the ethics of war should not percolate into peacetime. I then go on to suggest that adopting a raw utilitarian approach aids this unfortunate transition by using the simplistic arithmetic of utility to weigh up one person or group against another. The worst examples are a catalogue of lugubrious thought experiments in which one is put into an emergency situation and asked to make choices. Typically, the utilitarian mantra is used to encourage the saving of, say, ten people by sacrificing one.

The trolley example is perhaps the most famous.[41] We are allowed to play God and divert a trolley heading towards a group of workers to a side track where *only* a single person would be killed. This area of ethics, and there is a large body of literature on such conundrums, is one that this essay is pitted against. The ethics of emergency situations in peacetime seems like a proxy for wartime. Fortunately, there are authors who would share my views with responses such as these: Why do you put me in this artificial situation that does not treat people as human beings, but just as digits in a pseudo-ethical arithmetic? What if the single person is your sister, Mozart or just someone sun-bathing on holiday with no social connection with the situation?

One cannot just go round selecting innocent civilians to kill, whether or not this allows others to survive. That is the same logic as taking body parts from people in one (poor) country and shipping them to another (rich) country.

It's the idea of being placed in this situation, and asked to make the decisions with no semblance of reality, no narrative and no humanity that is the worst aspect of these problems. They are like advertisements for utilitarianism. I can see my antagonist, the pub expert on ethics, who wants to put me in a corner and, with their face up against mine, says, "Yes, but what would *you* do?" Behind the face, the only logic is that ten is bigger than one. Unfortunately, there are real emergency situations in which there are not enough resources, but that involve real people and real professionals trying to make good of a bad situation.

An example is what happened in Memorial Hospital in New Orleans in the height of the Hurricane Katrina disaster. In a detailed analysis in her book *Five Days at Memorial*, Sheri Fink pieces together the developing situations and the ad hoc rules that were developed where real people were sacrificed to save others.[42] Everything about this episode remains controversial: the failure of the helicopters to arrive; and the brutality, even arrogance, of the rules cooked up to sacrifice the sick and immobile to save the less sick and more mobile. Unlike the imagined lone victim in the trolley example, the victims' families sued and essentially won.

A critique of this essay could be that I have avoided addressing *self-sacrifice*. A full discussion would have to distinguish carefully between selfless and courageous action by an individual, and – like soldiers in a war in which the rules are determined by the leaders – out of necessity. Situations like Hurricane Katrina and the COVID-19 pandemic present difficult issues. In the early stages of the pandemic, doctors, nurses and other medical staff worked without full PPE and some died as a consequence. Without detracting from their great courage in any way, we could ask to what extent was public duty expected or additional moral pressure exerted. Would, for example, a nurse – who was already not well paid – feel or be told that they would lose their job if they did not turn up for work? Where does it say in their (peacetime) contract that they must put themselves at such risk? Very brave soldiers have deserted, and have even been shot for cowardice, even when they were the last one standing and they considered that their death was inevitable. Despite the extreme courage of the crews in Bomber Command in World War II (WW2) and the high chance of being killed on each sortie, the Royal Air Force still classified those who quit as having a "lack of moral fibre" (LMF), a vicious stigmatisation.[43]

There is one phrase, which is in a kind of grim sense of timing for me and a nightmare for us all, from an Italian doctor, who said in the teeth of the COVID-19 crisis, "I am having to choose who gets the ventilator." Without trying to claim any prescience and without any unwarranted drama, watching the doctor on television while personally in self-isolation was poignant at the very least. By then, I had already written that, in normal circumstances, not having enough intensive care units was *unacceptable*. It had never occurred to me that, shortly, there would not be enough ventilators, and sometimes not even enough oxygen, to cope with a pandemic. This is despite reports saying we were unprepared.[44] In the UK, we have had ex-ministers of health apologising for cutbacks in the NHS during the time of austerity. Not since WW2 have the forced choices been so stark. The UK government left itself precious little time to prepare for the pandemic. It had even less time to make us familiar with the choices it is responsible for and, as far as one can predict at the time of writing, preparing to blame the public for its own failings.

Now, just as in the New Orleans Memorial Hospital, a COVID-19 Decision Support Tool has been uncovered, which is to help the NHS choose who gets critical intensive care, and is based on a hybrid of utilitarian arithmetic and antiquated reverse-triage principles, namely that only those who are estimated to be saveable will be saved.[45] There was even talk of the old being sent home, possibly to die, based on an age cap. The idea of denying a treatment to one group because the probability of survival is less than for another group is the worst kind of raw utilitarian gobbledegook. It is also probably illegal, as it was for the Memorial Hospital victims. It surely cannot be a defence that the UK government failed to supply enough ventilators, because some messianic advisor thought he could push through eugenic principles incorporated in a crackpot theory about herd immunity. We will wait patiently for the court judgements, as we did for the ventilators. Meanwhile maybe famous professors of ethics may write papers with titles such as "Choice theories in the economics of oxygen supply".

One way in which we may find arithmetic of a utilitarian kind creeping into everyday life is where we give over the ethical decisions to automata. We shall see some of this in the use of drones in warfare in Chapter 9. In the comedy programme *Little Britain*, some poor claimant for a social service is faced with an official who responds to a quite reasonable request with, "Computer says no!" Worse even than panels involved willingly in WTP experiments to help underpin the social welfare functions of our public services is the idea that the utilitarian rules will be built into robots programmed to make life-and-death decisions.

We can imagine the well-funded research team that will design such monsters. Let us, in irony, help the multidisciplinary group that will write the grant application. Clearly, it will be useful to have an image-processing expert, and previous work on drones or surveillance would be an advantage to the applicants. Alongside the experts on artificial intelligence (AI) and machine learning (ML), we must have our token social scientist. Maybe if it's a project on autonomous vehicles, we can employ an urban sociologist who has expertise on how pedestrians behave. And then, of course, we need our ethicist. Here, a background in health economics or medical ethics would be useful. We don't want any wishy-washy religious or virtue theory type, and definitely not someone who witters on about human rights. We are engineers, for goodness' sake.

After writing that paragraph, I found an example called the Moral Machine, which – considering my comments on the trolley problem on which this Massachusetts Institute of Technology (MIT) project draws – can only be my worst nightmare.[46]

4.

Everyone has the same chance

Hardly a month goes by without a workshop on risk or uncertainty. Given the failures in areas such as banking, climate change and pandemics, with the possibility of repeats, this is not surprising. Understanding risk and uncertainty is also hard. It seems that virtually every academic discipline has something to say on the subject, and some have a real professional interest: economics, statistics and decision theory. There is also a spectrum from very theoretical risk theories (in, say, finance) to rather informal scoring methods (in risk control in industry).

Risk, at least, has a formal mathematical definition: risk = the probability of an event × the effect of that event. That seems simple. You toss a fair coin, and you win £100 if it comes up heads or nothing if it's tails. The expected gain is ½ × £100 = £50, and the expected loss is also £50. This expected loss we call the risk.

However, there are problems. The probability may be very small (we use the term "rare event") and the loss may be very large, and both may be very hard to measure. Catastrophes fall into this category. Another issue is that people may not actually behave in a way that minimises their risk, and the same amount of risk to a poor person may feel different to a rich person.

Probability is often separated into different types and two types dominate. The first is like the toss of a coin; in principle, the probability of achieving heads can be approximated very closely by tossing it a large number of times or by appealing to some kind of scientific or geometric symmetry. This is at the core of statistical theory. In some ways, the biased coin – one where the probability of heads is unknown – is a canonical problem in the theory.

The second type of probability is called "subjective", which is a word that opens a Pandora's box. Another term as frightening as subjective is "guess", and you can mix things up as in "My guess is that the probability of it snowing tomorrow is five percent". Most problematical is a subjective probability for something we may loosely call a "one-off event", or what some philosophers call a "contingent event". We are all proud of our favourite staggering coincidence. It takes a lot of hard work to convince ourselves that it may not be so staggering after all.

Uncertainty has a long but less celebrated history than probability theory and risk. Take the failure, or what is considered to be a failure by many writers, of probability to represent ignorance: "I really don't have any idea of the probability of the bent coin coming up heads, so please don't ask me to give a prior distribution!" or "If my keys are not on my desk, I don't know where they are." The word "uncertainty" has been used by Frank Knight to describe the black hole of ignorance that probability cannot describe.[47] Probability theory has strict axioms, whereas the handling of ignorance requires some weaker form of inference, logic or rationality. The jury is still out on such matters.

Gambling is a very important concept in the history of probability, in the foundations of game theory and even in the definition of subjective probability. It creeps into everyday life, in phrases such as "life is a gamble", "she took her chances" and "I wager that…"

Insurance is a gamble. When we agree to cover a £5,000 flood excess on a home in a flood zone, we are betting that it will not flood. It may be that the insurance company gives us no choice, forcing the gamble on us. A gamble in which everyone has the same chance of winning, such as a national lottery, seems fair. But even then one can think of ways in which it might not be fair. If there was a large group of gamblers who were disposed to choose the sequence 1, 2, 3, 4, 5, 6 every time, then they would each have the same chance of winning but if the rules require that a fixed jackpot has to be split, the expected gain (the negative of risk) would be less.

Let us return to ethics and a version of ethics based on some idea of equity, which we have alluded to previously. What I will try to unravel and argue against is the kind of situation in which the phrase "everyone has the same risk" is used to claim fairness for a policy before an event. It's a question of before and after. Within a specific demographic category, one may say that everyone has the same chance of getting some particular life-threatening disease. However, for the person who gets the disease, can it be fair? Indeed, is life fair? Of course it's not! Is it fair to be born into a poor family in a ward in the UK with a life expectancy that is around ten years less than being born into a rich ward?

There is no harm in calculating and developing theories of risk. Indeed, it's an essential part of any field in which there can be serious loss or gain. What is wrong is to confuse and equate risk with equality. This may seem strange at first. After all, unequal risk – as with the example of birth – is certainly an indicator of inequality. But the use of risk to give a semblance of equity before an event should be distinguished from real inequity after the event. The distinction is often lost by decision-makers in government and industry.

To put it more accurately, the failure to mention or predict the variation in the outcome can be used to give a misleading idea of equality and, at worst, may be using probability as a smokescreen. Using a simple average or mean is very close to a raw utilitarian approach. Advertising that the probability of death for a large population is small means a large proportion of non-deaths, which is very close to the greatest good for the greatest number. This fuzziness is also dangerous if it is the end of the matter, because failure to acknowledge the inequity in the outcome may discourage the search for a better outcome; for example, a safer vaccine.

Gambling is one of the world's biggest businesses. The annual global turnover from all types of gambling is estimated at around $500 billion. Gambling is available on the internet at any time of day or night. In addition to normal gambling, there is the stock market. Although it is a vital part of generating investment capital for industry, most people would see the stock market as a form of gambling. The distaste for investment banking following the 2008 financial meltdown is summarised by people thinking, correctly, of the investment banks and funds as gambling with other people's money. This has led to moves to split the retail side of banking from the investment side or to have firewalls of some kind between the two.

Ordinary gambling and, one imagines, gambling on the stock market, is addictive and can lead to serious social problems. A study in Australia, where the issue is taken very seriously, estimates that around one percent of the whole population have a gambling problem.[48] A strong argument against gambling is that the worst social consequences arise with those – typically, the poor – who can ill-afford to gamble. Gambling sells a hope. A win gives a short-term reinforcement, but gambling in the long run can lead to ruin. In Japan, I was told privately, gambling machines may be tuned so that with a long use of a particular machine a person can actually gain a slight advantage by learning the favourable patterns. Nevertheless, most people do not have the time to get to the point of advantage, and someone else may be monopolising their favourite machine.

Along with the ethos of gambling, chance and probability are better understood and increasingly (excuse the pun) part of common currency. There is an acceptance that there will be winners and losers. After all, if you do not accept the possibility of losing, you would not gamble. Acceptance serves the interests of the gaming industry in terms of profits and of the government as it extracts taxes on gambling.

The public appreciation of risk requires some understanding of simple probability, or at least of orders of magnitude. There are problems; for example, in getting the denominator right in calculating rates. Should one measure transport risk per journey, per kilometre or per hour? There is the risk of an accident, but then there is the accident itself. There is accident prevention, and there is emergency action. These are not the same thing. There is probability, and there is an event. In fact, an event can change the probability of another event, which is the basis for extensive theories of causation. If it rains today, it is more likely to flood. We find this contrast between the risk and the event quite often. When just after a train or a plane accident, the company declares, "We have one of the best safety records", the news item grates for the listener and must seem like some kind of sick joke to the victims' families.

To summarise, the understanding and appreciation of the risks of events by the public should not be used as a vehicle to obtain acceptance of the consequences via a false sense of equity. There are winners and losers, but it need not be like that. For the gambling company – and for the hedge fund, of course – there must be winners and losers. They profit from the wheel of fortune. An academic economist, particularly one working on the more probabilistic wing of the subject, understands that – in a fair market, or a perfect market – neither seller nor buyer should lose. At the point of exchange, both parties are happy. However, in actual markets, there are big winners and big losers, as big as banks and even countries.

There is one way in which probability distributions in the mathematical sense are distinct from distributions in the population sense. This ambivalence is built in to statistical inference. In many contexts, we discuss the background population from which a sample is taken and from which internal population parameters can be estimated, such as a mean or standard deviation. In mathematical statistics, we make idealised assumptions about the population distribution such that it is a normal (Gaussian) distribution or is from some other famous family of distributions. Even in areas such as nonparametric statistics, one can still have an idealised distribution in this way, though they may fall into a more flexible, adaptable family. This dichotomy between real-but-finite populations and theoretical distributions persists, and it is often confusing to students. The student who is used to mathematical abstraction may be happy to assume a nice background population distribution. Also, in areas such as statistical physics where there may be an extremely large population of interacting particles, such idealisations are inherent in the topic. Conversely, in the social sciences, there is less bravado about making such assumptions.

An income distribution is the distribution of real people with real incomes. It may be that medium incomes are well modelled by the lognormal distribution, and high incomes by the Pareto distribution, but with real-life distributions, any use of the term "probability" requires a thought experiment. Thus we may decide to select a person at random from the finite population, and with a probability of one-half, their income will be above £30,000 a year.

But we must not overstretch this thought experiment by talking about someone's "bad luck" at being born into a family with a low income. This confuses structural inequalities in a real population with some hypothetical game of chance played by the goddess Fate. Probability should not be used in this way to mask inequality. In the same way, treating a financial elite holding a high percentage of the world's wealth as the result of some unalterable fundamental process is not acceptable. Given the failure of free-market economics to reduce inequalities, and supposing one could find a satisfying economic theory that could explain income inequality, it would not be acceptable to set that theory in stone, like a law of physics, even if it has – and maybe particularly if it has – probabilistic principles embedded in it. Even physicists have the sense to think that their most cherished fundamental laws may one day need to be abandoned, if they make a mathematical mistake or if the raw data is really stacked against them.

The insurance industry knows all about equity. It likes to collect as much information as it can afford about its customers, so that it can design contracts to make money. Sometimes, it is banned from discriminating, such as in the European ruling against the use of gender. At the same time, it likes to spread risk so that it can offer attractive contracts over a wider population and capture a good proportion of the market. One solution is to offer standard contracts, backed by exemptions.

It seems to me that there is a close link between some aspects of modern finance and the use of probability as a kind of moral camouflage. Some of the ethical essence is contained in the single word "arbitrage". Here is an example, with apologies for forgetting my source. I buy cheaply and drink some bottles of beer in country A, which has a border with country B. I take the empty bottles over the border to country B and get cash in return for the empty bottles. I then take the cash back over the border to country A, where it is enough to buy the same quantity of beer. This gives me an endless source of beer in return for the small initial investment. There is, of course, a transaction cost in tramping over the border with my bottles clinking in my backpack, but we will ignore this.

Arbitrage has several slightly different definitions, but, essentially, it arises where differences in price indicate an imperfect market of some kind, out of which – as with the beer – we can make a profit. Information is critical to making this profit. As the only person on the border who is aware of the empty bottle scam, I can carry on regardless. But the truth may out. My drinking partners, the border guards, the beer sellers and the bottle bank may find me out eventually.

Statistical arbitrage combined with fast trading is used to exploit short-term arbitrage advantages. If the same information is available to all, then this may be seen as a kind of fair gambling, but there may be advantages based on different levels of access to market information, different speeds of computer and connection, and so on. It seems that the boundary between statistical arbitrage and insider dealing is foggy. The regulators, particularly the US Security and Exchange Commission, are continually patrolling the boundary with varying degrees of success. Returning again to the beer example: by not telling anyone what I am doing, am I essentially stealing or simply exploiting a bit of information that I came across by chance? When does arbitrage become theft?[49]

Most legal jurisdictions require you to take reasonable measures to find the owner of something you found by accident, such as a wad of bank notes dropped in the street. If the money is in a wallet, with identification such as a credit card, then the situation is clear: you must return the money. But even if there is no identification you are typically required to take the money to a police station, although there may be a time limit for a claim to be made by the real owner.

Many will recall the huge pleasure in finding that one's lost property has been handed in anonymously: it restores our faith in humanity. It is an antidote to the raw ethics of the playground contained in the phrase "finders keepers, losers weepers" – the ethics of arbitrage. There are winners and losers: the losers are like the child in the corner of the playground, feeling upset and a little stupid for having dropped their favourite silver sixpence. And perhaps the upset child is the patient who is upset because, in the lottery of life, she has lost not a coin but her health. If we do not treat her for cost reasons, someone else benefits from saving that expense. This would be like finding her £100 in the street and giving it to someone else. The cynicism of the beer drinker, the financial market trader, and the pupil who found the child's silver sixpence and did not hand it to the teacher is little different in my mind from the cynicism of the local CCGs in the UK who declare that the new drug has been "disinvested" in for "rational" reasons.

What I am objecting to is the transfer into every corner of public life of the raw gambling attitude to probability and risk that implies there must be winners and losers. We may gamble on stocks and shares, and on the Grand National horse race, but we don't want to be gambling when we breathe the air in the city we live in, or when we cross the road carefully: "Head before feet when you cross the street". Measuring risk, the perception of risk and learning better to appreciate risk, though all important, must never be taken as an acceptance of risk, any more than helping people cope with poverty or disability means that we should accept poverty or disability and the processes that cause them. Acknowledgement and care are not the same as acceptance. To repeat, understanding risk before an event should never be used to make light of a bad outcome if it occurs. That would be like an insurance company advertising a fair premium but never paying a claim.

A question at the frontier of social justice and the free market, which arises from scientific progress, is this: should insurance companies have access to biometric data on individuals, particularly genomic data? From a commercial perspective, and this is certainly free-market thinking, it is the duty of an insurance company to maximise profits for shareholders, and separating risk into different categories and levels (risk classification) may help in this direction, particularly if the company can thereby get a competitive advantage. However, genetic testing is fraught with problems. The predictive power of the models may be so weak that it is not worth the administrative and statistical effort to extract the advantage. There may also be useful information about not only the immediate customer but the whole family. If asking for genetic information from tests on an individual is already a breach of privacy, asking for information from third parties is even more of one. Furthermore, although insurance mathematics and statistics have become much more sophisticated, they may still lack the highly sophisticated scientific methods used in modern bioinformatics. For these reasons, it is likely that the insurance company will concentrate on diseases that have higher mortality rates and for which the profile is clearly identifiable. Allowing insurance companies access to gene data allows them to discriminate. In some countries, the use of gene data in insurance is banned, in others it is allowed, and in yet others still some kind of voluntary agreement has been reached, such as the Association of British Insurers' concordat (ABI) in the UK.[50]

One school of thought says that the classical basis of insurance was a mutuality in which risks are pooled so that the "lucky" ones in the pool would pay for the "unlucky" ones. This is the foundation for social insurance, and one view is that insurance companies ought still to live by this rule. We can see the dilemma. There are perceived commercial opportunities from using the new kinds of data combined with an array of methodologies from statistics and computer science, but precisely by concentrating on individual information, there is a danger of incubating new types of discrimination and thus new forms of sacrifice. If an insurance company classifies people into pools of ever-decreasing size, then for those in high-risk pools, the personal insurance provided may be prohibitively expensive. If the state refuses to pick up the cost because of some kind of cost-per-QALY cap, then that is absolute discrimination and the creation of a neglected sacrificial pool. If the risk arises from genetic disorders, then this would, *de facto*, be a modern type of eugenics. At least flood victims may have the opportunity to move to safer areas.

Perhaps the most insidious version of the life-equals-money equations in the utilitarian language used in health and safety is the notion of the value of a statistical life (VSL), which was used first in transport safety. VSL hides behind marginal effects: if the probability of surviving for a period such as one year is p and the monetary value of surviving the period is w, then the VSL is the marginal rate expressed as a differential, dw/dp. Many technical objections have been raised: difficulties with heterogeneous populations, with different levels of risk aversion and favouring the rich because they have more wealth to lose if they die.

Nevertheless, one critique stands out. A version of the so-called "Broome paradox" is very close to the critique of risk in this chapter, namely that statistical risk hides itself behind anonymity. Since we don't know who is going to die, we are in a situation just like an insurance pool, but without the built-in mutuality, even altruism, of such a pool. VSL says nothing about the individual. The Broome paradox declares that if the victim is identifiable, then they would seek massive compensation, and the whole risk analysis project would have to be abandoned.[51] This is precisely the distinction between identifiability and non-identifiability, which we have mentioned before, and is clearly morally false. The fact that we do not know who is going to suffer ought to be entirely independent of the moral wrong. The danger is that concepts such as VSL and value of a statistical life year (VSLY) – which are defined using small, marginal effects – are then used in safety studies, under a heading of "the risk method", to define thresholds for *in*action. The UK HSE explains in its *ALARP at a Glance*:

> *In essence, making sure a risk has been reduced under ALARP is about weighing the risk against the sacrifice by the company, needed to further reduce it. The decision should be weighted in favour of health and safety because the presumption is that the duty-holder should implement the risk reduction measure. To avoid having to make this sacrifice, the duty-holder must be*

> *able to show that it would be grossly disproportionate to the*
> *benefits of risk reduction that would be achieved. Thus, the*
> *process is not one of balancing the costs and benefits of measures*
> *but, rather, of adopting measures except where they are ruled*
> *out because they involve grossly disproportionate 'sacrifices'.*[52]

It is when VSL is used to define the threshold over which a company need *not* invest in safety that we find that we are back in the steep and icy ethical landscape of QALYs. VSL employed to make incremental decisions about investment in safety is one thing, but using it to define thresholds in technical areas that may particularly affect small groups of workers is like denying certain patients specific drugs.

In the aforementioned HSE summary, we note the distasteful co-option of the word "sacrifice", twice in a paragraph, but on the side of the company; the phrase "grossly disproportionate sacrifices" is now part of the language, but with the company making the "sacrifices".

Statins are a worldwide business exceeding £30 billion. The cardiovascular disease (CVD) risk score is the percentage probability that you will contract the disease in the next ten years. If the score is 25%, this probability is one-quarter. People are prescribed statins to reduce this risk. There is some evidence that people in high-risk groups benefit, although this evidence is still somewhat controversial, and it is very controversial as to whether people in low-risk groups benefit at all. There is also emerging evidence of side effects. The clinical trials have been poor at measuring side effects such as muscle pain and damage, liver damage and diabetes, and there are accusations about side effects being hidden. There is also much anecdotal evidence from GPs and patients of the kind "When my mother stopped taking statins, she felt a lot better."

Let us consider the logic of giving low-risk patients statins by taking two extreme cases. The first, which I will call the "lottery model", is that there is only a small group of patients who benefit, but we do not really know who they are. In that case, taking statins is to take a gamble that you are in the group that will benefit. The gamble costs you nothing if you get the drug on the NHS – except, of course, that you may contribute via taxation to the total NHS bill for statins, which is huge. The other model is that everyone in the low-risk group benefits physiologically to some extent. This would be similar to losing weight, daily exercise, better diet, etc. We might call this second model the "universal model".

The lottery model has deep ethical and practical implications. It means that statins are no better than a placebo for most people in the lowest group. Actually, they would be worse off because of possible side effects. It may even be that you are in a group for which there is an increased risk of CVD. It is very disturbing that if the lottery model is correct, the drug companies have a motive *not* to find out how to describe the small group that would benefit, because that would undermine the message that they are beneficial for all, and hence negatively affect the huge sales. It seems to me that that they are selling the universal model.

The confusion between the lottery model and universal model is a reverse version of the Broome paradox: we object to selling a universal probability of benefit if, in fact, only small groups will actually benefit. It is no justification that we do not know what those groups are. To put it as bluntly as we can: there is no financial motive to target the drug if everyone is persuaded to take it in any case. The battle rages on: effect versus no effects, hidden side effects, undue pressure on doctors and regulators, lawsuits, big headlines on both sides and internecine warfare in the medical journals.

The sentiment that there must be winners and losers casts society and life as being a vast game, and as we have seen here, it is a game of chance. It is not a surprise to find that many of the theories of economics that include some kind of probability are seen as an aspect of game theory. There are games such as zero-sum (what you win, I lose), cooperative games, games with imperfect information, dynamic games and so on. The thrust of this essay is contained in the blunt quotation from the Stanford Encyclopedia of Philosophy:

> *Agents who wish to avoid inefficient outcomes are best advised to prevent certain games from arising; the defender of the possibility of Kantian rationality is really proposing that they try to dig themselves out of such games by turning themselves into different kinds of agents.*[53]

The point is that if each of us is trying to maximise our own utility, then we are driven towards the cynical universality of "life's a game of chance".

I like mathematics, mathematical statistics and optimisation. I like the decision-theoretic paradigm that statistics is a game against a Mother Nature whose secrets are hard to find. However, and this should be clear from my remarks about health economics in Chapter 2, I abhor mathematics being used to add an extra halo of mystique to decent and useful work. Yes, it is true: I did indeed steal the first word of my title from Feyerabend's *Against Method*, in which he argues against the domination of method and the deliberate mystification that it can lead to.[54] Method and mathematics can be seductive. The geometric wings of mathematics have a hallucinatory quality that is not just close to art but some say *is* art. Put the words "geometric" and "topological" before any field, and you inspire admiration: geometric measure theory or topological data analysis. Algebraic geometry is a huge slice of mathematics. Add the word "quantum", and you are in the big time. Game theory has the same glamour. But we are with Feyerabend: "Progress has always been achieved by probing well-entrenched and well-founded forms of life with unpopular and unfounded values. This is how man gradually freed himself from fear and from the tyranny of unexamined systems."

Common decency or sheer embarrassment will stop any minister of health saying that the NHS is playing games with people's lives, but a cursory look shows that game theory has crept into health economics. The same is true for rationality, where that rationality means how best to maximise someone's utility. You can find game theory in construction safety, and there is at least one paper describing a three-player game: customer, company and regulator.

We should return again to the issue of risk. The term dominates policy, typically with bland remarks such as "We have followed a risk-based approach", "The risk of buying this pension scheme was explained", "The consultant has explained the risk to the patient", and "The risk of dying of COVID-19 is minute if you are young, compared to if you are old". All this seems very uncontroversial. What could possibly go wrong? We hope to have explained previously what is wrong, but let's do it one more time.

It is the very blandness that should make us suspicious. The risk-based approach seems like a kind of safety blanket hiding all kinds of hidden iniquities and inequities. You could reply to any of the prior statements with the sarcastic statement, "I see, so that's all right then," and wait for the response. Ask "Did you include the long-term effects of COVID-19 in your risk analysis?", "Has your risk analysis been approved by the regulator?", and "Do you have patients/students/homeless/women/customers/pensioners on your risk committee?". We need risk analysis, and whether we like it or not, it is here to stay. But we also need to be very forensic in our understanding of it. We need to be clear whom it is who is disbenefitted if something goes wrong; we need to hear their voices, their side of the story.

5.

For the public good

Although vaccination benefits the individual, it also benefits the community. In the case of whooping cough, young children are vaccinated only partly for their own benefit. They are vaccinated mainly for society's sake, and especially for the sake of siblings. It is because they are wounded in the war against disease, a battle fought on behalf of the whole community, that this small group of children should be compensated.[55]

Jack Ashley

One of the most controversial issues that has set families against governments is that of vaccination. There is no doubt that vaccination has been one of medicine's greatest contributions to human health, and it is one of the major responsibilities of primary care; that is to say, local clinics and GP services. Typically, the aim is to have every young child vaccinated against mumps, measles, rubella, whooping cough and chickenpox. Epidemics are tough to control. If not enough people are vaccinated, then the infection rates will be too high, and there could be epidemics in which children and adults will suffer and even die. The incidence of diseases, the infection rates, the way the epidemics move through populations, the ebb and flow of the epidemics, and the way that different strains emerge and interact are all part of the subject of epidemiology. If one had to bet what might eventually eliminate the human race, or a good part of it, a pandemic with no adequate vaccine, or an inadequate supply of vaccines and antiviral drugs would be high up many people's lists, alongside nuclear war and climate change. Epidemics are on the list of horrors on the politician's desk.

Nonetheless, there are side effects to vaccination. The size and even the existence of side effects is often disputed, and governments can get locked into arguments with those who consider themselves or a family member to have been adversely affected. We should have no doubt that a child who dies or who is brain damaged by a vaccine is sacrificed for the public good. And we should not hide behind the fact that the chance of any particular child being a victim is very small and say that vaccination is fair. Vaccination is palpably *not* fair. If it's your child who is damaged, it is no good saying that it *was* fair. Neither should we hide behind "genetic disposition" or any other post hoc arguments. This is a version of blaming the victim, which I will say more about in Chapter 8.

Driven by the public-good argument, the pressure on families to have their children vaccinated is intense. There is a lot to be said about the ethics of vaccination and the motivation behind state compulsion (mandate) to vaccinate. First, one may ask whether the compulsion comes from concern for each individual or for the population. One teaches a child to put their "head before feet when you cross the street" because of the risk to the individual child – *your* child. Road accidents are not infectious. But with vaccination, there is the additional argument that if not enough children are vaccinated, there could be an epidemic. It is this second argument that dominates. A parent who refuses to have their child vaccinated is being selfish in putting the population at risk. From the standpoint of ethics, this is a fundamental utilitarian argument: the greatest good is to vaccinate all. Refusal is only admonished in the UK, but the penalties are severe in some other countries.

The side effects and the fear of them have generated pressure groups to lobby for change. Powerful, ethical arguments are used on both sides. We now have the notorious "anti-vax movement". Perhaps the most dramatic argument is based on the reference to the section of the Nuremberg Code that relates to consent in medical treatment, which arose out of the forcible medical treatment of concentration camp victims by Nazi doctors. The first point of the code says this:

> *The voluntary consent of the human subject is absolutely essential. This means that the person involved should have the legal capacity to give consent; should be situated in a manner as to be able to exercise free power of choice, without intervention of force, fraud, duress, over-reaching or other ulterior forms of constraint or coercion. They should also have sufficient knowledge and comprehension of the elements of the subject matter involved as to enable him/her to make an understanding and enlightened decision.*[56]

The long, hard fight to get compensation for vaccination damage in the UK is told in the harrowing book *Helen's Story* by Rosemary Fox.[57] Her daughter Helen had been damaged by the polio vaccination in 1962. It is not our job here to relive this painful story, but we can draw lessons from it with regard to the relationship between individuals who feel wronged and the government acting in the general public interest. History is important. It is not good enough for politicians today to say that we are now in an improved situation when, at the same time, the institutions of Parliament and the civil service remain very much the same in terms of secrecy and regard for the individual. We cannot allow such events to be forgotten. It is important to study the attitudes of governments and the judiciary. Why was it, for example, that the compensation was so hard to extract and that the legal barriers were placed so high?

A group called Unit 73 – with the help of some academics and a large body of evidence, including letters from parents – persuaded Jack Ashley to take up the cause, and he managed to get Parliament to debate this. On 5 February 1979, he made the passionate speech in the House of Commons from which I gave a short extract previously. The formation of the Association of Parents of the Vaccine Damaged Children, the momentum generated by Jack Ashley's speech and much further campaigning led eventually to an award of up to £10,000 for victims whose families made successful applications.

The real scandal of this episode in British public life is the sheer length of time it took to fulfil these promises made in 1979 that would lead to a fully fledged compensation scheme. Germany has had such a scheme since 1962, and several other countries followed. It was not until 27 June 2000, some twenty-six years after Ashley's speech in 1974, that Chancellor Alistair Darling announced that the vaccination-damage payment would be increased to £100,000 for new cases and topped up for existing ones. It now stands as a maximum one-off payment of £120,000. However, the following is found:

Unfortunately, far from conveying the message of a scheme which is receptive and responsive in providing monetary

assistance to affected children and their families, the statistics
paint a picture of a scheme which more times than not,
refuses applications from vaccine damaged individuals. Since
its inception, a total of 6,026 have been submitted under the
Association of Parents of the Vaccine Damage Payments Act
1979 with only a mere 931 awards being made.[58]

It is one thing to argue that, in each of the particular cases, the brain damage was not caused by the vaccination, but it is quite another one for a judge to pronounce that there is no scientific connection at all, which happened along the way to getting compensation. In the US, cases were hampered by the meanness of the Legal Aid Board, and in the UK, cutbacks in state funding have led to legal aid in relation to the Vaccination Compensation Scheme being specifically excluded. The floodgates are closed. In the US, the National Vaccine Injury Compensation Program (NVICP) was introduced in 1998, and, since then, any liability of the drug companies for vaccination damage has been removed gradually after a long series of court battles. Finally, on 22 February 2011, the US Supreme Court shielded drug companies from all liability for harm caused by vaccinations mandated by government. From now on, drug companies selling vaccines in the US will not be held accountable by a jury of peers in a court of law. If you get paralysed by a flu shot or your child has a serious reaction to a vaccine (which is required in some states of the US to be granted a school place) and becomes learning disabled, epileptic, autistic, asthmatic, diabetic or develops a learning difficulty, then you are on your own.

At the same time, the element of compulsion to have your child vaccinated is increasing. The US Center for Disease Control (CDC) is in charge of the rules that govern compulsion, along with the individual US states. Some states do allow exemptions on religious grounds, and although these cases are rare, arguments are sometimes extended to include philosophical grounds of the kind studied in this essay. This makes for very interesting discussions and judgements that cover the tension between the liberty of the individual and the public or societal good. For serious infectious diseases, the full power of the law, including the use of police, is being folded into the CDC's rules, and whether this will be extended to the routine vaccination of children is not yet clear, although there is already much consternation. In the UK, we all relearned the meaning of the word "mandate" in the question of whether COVID-19 vaccination will be made compulsory.

The NVICP has also come under fire. It has built up a Vaccination Injury Trust that is worth several billion dollars, funded by a levy on the drug companies. It is criticised for its bureaucratic hurdles, time limits, long delays and miserly payouts. One good feature, though, is that the standards of proof have come down from having to establish scientific causation to just "the balance of probabilities". So, for cases in which the child is very young and the bad reaction was very swift, more complex causation proof is not required. As in the UK, the causal links with the whooping cough vaccine have been admitted, but the measles, mumps and rubella (MMR) vaccine's link to autism has been eliminated, although there is still agonising debate here and there.[59]

Despite some of the relaxation in the US, one of the crafty ways for a government – or its legal representatives – to argue against compensation, both in individual cases and in actual law and legal judgement, is to demand a particularly high level of proof of causation. The theory of causation is an important topic in the philosophy of science and what may loosely be called "methodology". Following the celebrated work by Judea Pearl, it is now a very active sub-branch of statistics, AI and data-driven areas of computer science such as ML. However, it remains fraught with difficult philosophical and mathematical problems. One philosophical problem is the use of subjective judgement (Bayesian methods), where expert judgement mingles with real data to update the assessment of causal effects. There are other generally agreed problems. One is that the association, or correlation, between events does not imply causation, although it may support it. Causation without correlation would be hard to argue. It is the requirement for the statistical evidence of an effect that pushes up sample sizes in clinical trials.

A less problematical issue is whether, for A to cause B, A must happen before B. It is agreed that it must. A strong version of the requirements to establish causation is intervention: if we apply drug A, there is an effect in contrast to not applying A (or a control). Some experts make intervention a strong requirement (which would make causation hard to discuss where there is non-human intervention). The burden of proof in a court of law is not very far from this strong requirement. But the law asks juries to weigh up the evidence in serious cases, although these juries do not know the theories of causation. A very strong requirement, particularly for newly observed outcomes, is to exhibit some causal mechanism. It helps to move from association to causation if some mechanism can be found to explain the link, but it would be bad science to throw away simple associations because a causation mechanism is *not* immediately apparent. Good science would be to look for a mechanism, or even set up a new research programme to look for a mechanism.

Into this maze of theories walk the parents of the (possibly) vaccine-damaged child. At the extreme, their judgements are set against those of a platoon of experts, both legal and scientific, demanding a high standard of proof. The deck is stacked against the parents. At the centre is the fact that there may be no causal mechanism established to explain the side effects, and no research programme to find it. Second, against the experts, the judgement of the parents may seem biased and non-scientific. Third, the standards of proof may be at least as high as those in obtaining a criminal conviction.

In a less one-sided debate, there ought to be a way to take into account the experience of the parents. One point is that there was indeed an intervention: the vaccination itself. Second, the effect is sometimes quite swift. There ought to be a way of according a high weighting to evidence in the form of "I took my child to the doctor in the morning, and by the evening, she was vomiting, would not eat and had a high fever, and she was never the same after that." Parents know things, and their intuition is intensely valuable. It is not just that A happens before B – the proximity of A to B may be critical. There are complicated arguments to be made about whether the nature of B is unusual and whether B came on swiftly or not.

Therefore, the current situation regarding vaccination, the laws and regulations relating to vaccination, and the compensation for damage, are in a varying degree of mess, depending on which country or state you live in. It is complicated by the fine balance between the public good and the side effects. On the side of public good, there are powerful forces: the government, the drug companies, the medical profession (mostly) and the moral force of those who willingly take their children to be vaccinated. Vaccination is an archetypal case in which individuals may be sacrificed for the public good. We should all be in favour of vaccination; I *am* in favour of vaccination. I am absolutely *not* anti-vax. This is a public good for all politicians, left and right. However, the view taken here is that – with respect to the use of compulsion – the failure to convey the true risks (the person-centred risks); the failure to acknowledge the side effects properly; and the failure to pay adequate compensation, and to pay it quickly and without restriction – none of that is in the public good. It creates opposition and a dark pool of bitterness. It is counterproductive, and it creates a climate of fear and suspicion that will, in the long run, help to diminish the actual vaccination rate, with bad consequences.

Among all the "crimes" of the powerful in this regard, perhaps complacency is the worst: the sentiment that says that things are all right as they are, and that the side-effect rates are acceptable. No policy in peacetime that sacrifices some citizens for the public good of the majority is acceptable. It may be a necessary evil in the short term, but side effects should be the spur to look for a safer alternative. We shall say later that these hard choices are precisely where the ethical effort, the attention and the funding should be placed. Good risk theory tells us not only to mitigate the effects but also to prevent the adverse events and hard choices in future.

A maxim at the foundation of the legal system is that no one is above the law, and that should include the government itself. This allows individuals, in theory, to sue the government for damages caused by its negligence or any criminal behaviour. In practice, this is bound up in a complicated area of jurisprudence that is referred to variously as "administrative liability" or "administrative tort". In practice, in order to obtain damages, very high standards of proof are required. The alleged victim has to show that the actions of the government were truly negligent and also to establish some kind of causal chain leading to the adverse event, and all this in the situation of informational asymmetry. As has already been said, the government is able to command an army of experts, whereas the individual citizen may not even have access to legal aid.

But the cases I am interested in are those where the state acts, or thinks it acts, in the public interest. This operates at two levels. In specific cases, the state uses the defence of *necessity*. A famous example is where the house of an innocent person had to be destroyed to help block the path of the great San Francisco fire.[60] Another might be where an innocent bystander is caught in the crossfire from a police action. In these cases, most administrations will give compensation.

However, it becomes harder when, as with vaccination, there is some large-scale societal good in which a small minority of innocent citizens are adversely affected. One issue is where the government provides the motivation, but the root cause of the damage is provided by a third party. This is exactly the case with vaccination. The government encourages and cajoles parents to take their children to be vaccinated, but the damage is caused by the vaccination itself. The cajoling may be part of a declared public policy or part of a more clandestine "nudging" campaign. I personally prefer a more traditional and honest health education approach: "Take this pill; it will do you good."

One very effective way of handling these issues is to introduce a no-blame system. This has worked well in the medical area. In New Zealand, such a system was introduced and has continually been reviewed and improved. The disadvantage for the claimant is that damages are more or less fixed according to the severity, so that very large damages are not possible, although most systems have some kind of loophole allowing individuals to carry out separate legal actions if they insist. The advantage is that cases can be dealt with quickly, with lower legal costs and with milder standards of proof.

In France, state liability was introduced in 1895. There *responsibilité pour risqué* (liability for risk), is based partly on principles of equality: *responsibilité pour rupture de l'egalité devant les charges publiques* (liability for breach of equality of public offices). In Germany, there is a long-established principle of "*Sonderopfer*" (special sacrifice),[61] which states that if the effect is more than what might normally be expected for its citizens, you should be compensated. Although there are similar laws in other EU countries, the European Commission has avoided embodying these ideas into any directive to date, although there is a body of case law.

In the UK, the Law Commission published a report and held a consultation exercise that led to mild suggestions covering much of the ground in other countries' legislation, including pointing out the problems of resources. But other than a promise to take more notice of the issue via departments and ombudsmen, the whole question was promptly shelved by the UK government:

> *This project was notable in that the key stakeholder – the Government – was firmly opposed to our proposed reforms. This opposition was expressed both in the formal response and in discussions at both ministerial and official level. Government's formal response was a single document agreed across Government. This is extremely unusual, if not unique, in recent times.*[62]

So, in the UK, that's the end of that.

In economics, influences that are divorced from those captured by a particular transaction or contractual environment are called "externalities". Positive externalities are typically those outside a real or hypothetical main contract. A change from diesel to electric buses in a city will benefit all citizens because it will lower pollution. A negative externality would arise from a new, unclean coal-fired power station. There is much classical economic theory related to externalities. Whole subjects, such as CBA, are based on the acknowledgement of externalities. As this essay is being written, the decision whether to build a new runway at Heathrow may be affected by the fact that pollution levels in the area exceed the EU limits. However, in both the legal and economic analysis, the damage to individuals is underplayed. It seems that the main contract is always at centre stage, including the public good, the commitment to the commercial need for a new runway, and so on. This bias creeps into the terminology: side effects, collateral damage and externalities all seem like afterthoughts. If a child has an asthma attack or worse, then describing it as an externality seems to me like an insult. The child is one of us. She lives among us. She goes to the same doctor. The air she breathes is all around us and is in our own lungs too. This is as far from being an externality as could be.

6.

Duty of care

What do we expect our elected representatives and the government run by them to do? We certainly hope that they look after the common good, both for our own citizens and those of other countries, and refrain from feathering their own nests. I believe they should have a well-established duty of care to each and every citizen and visitor. They should not just measure their success by some macro-utilitarian measure, such as so many hospital beds for so much money. Footballers are encouraged to play together as a team, and a good manager will be attentive to the health, training and so on of each player. A government has responsibility to the gross domestic product (GDP), the national debt, the overall literacy and all the macro measures (the political equivalent of winning the football game). However, they should have the imagination to understand that they have a duty of care, and just like the good football manager, they should be able to look us in the eye, tell us so and mean it, and not just when they shake our hand during an election campaign.

The rule that you are to love your neighbour translates in law to the fact that you must not injure your neighbour, and the legal question of who your neighbour is receives a restricted reply at the moment. You must take reasonable care to avoid acts or omissions that you can reasonably foresee would be likely to injure your neighbour. The answer seems to be that your neighbours are persons who are so closely and directly affected by you that you ought reasonably to have them in contemplation as being so affected when directing your mind to the acts or omissions that are called into question. Thus, a duty of care includes the idea of "proximity". A driver has a duty of care, not just to their passengers but also to pedestrians.

Now, those in positions of power who affect our lives on a day-to-day basis are proximate in a very real sense. The National Grid can have a power cut (outage) such that the lights go out. That is proximate from an electro-dynamic point of view. Utility contracts may deliberately exclude a duty to provide a continuous supply of what they should be supplying, which is typically to avoid compensation or litigation. We can argue that the more powerful the organisation, the greater should be their duty of care, not less. Nonetheless, the powerful have ways of wriggling out of what could be seen as obligation: they simply remove the litigation risk in the small print.

Miraculously, the Dutch courts have made use of duty of care in an environment case: the Urgenda case. The Dutch court ruled thus:

> *The question whether the State is in breach of its duty of care for taking insufficient measures to prevent dangerous climate change, is a legal issue which has never before been answered in Dutch proceedings and for which jurisprudence does not provide a ready-made framework. The answer to the question whether or not the State is taking sufficient mitigation measures depends on many factors, with two aspects having particular*

relevance. In the first place, it has to be assessed whether there is an unlawful hazardous negligence on the part of the State. Secondly, the State's discretionary power is relevant in assessing the government's actions. From case law about government liability it follows that the court has to assess fully whether or not the State has exercised or exercises sufficient care, but that this does not alter the fact that the State has the discretion to determine how it fulfills its duty of care. However, this discretionary power vested in the State is not unlimited: the State's care may not be below standard. However, the test of due care required here and the discretionary power of the State are not wholly distinguishable. After all, the detailing of the duty of care of the person called to account will also have been included in his specific position in view of the special nature of his duty or authority. The standard of care has been attuned to this accordingly.[63]

This judgement has received much acclaim, probably because it is a rare case of a nation getting to grips with the issue of duty of care, with careful argument, and that contains an acknowledgement of the duty and a warning that it requires standards within which discretion must operate.

Two tests apply in this essay for whether I think that a government takes its duty of care seriously, which is whether it pays adequate compensation for those it sacrifices for the public good and whether it tries to minimise hard choices. In a way, the state has it both ways. It can decide when it needs to nudge or coerce the public into certain actions, such as vaccination, but then it surely has a duty in those situations; for example, to pay compensation. However, two things can happen. First, it may not actually pay compensation, despite the administrative-tort arguments, and, second, the choice of when to use the public-good argument gives the state the power to be selective. The Dutch case is a warning that the state cannot just pick and choose when it should exercise duty of care.

Take as an example the duty of care to ensure that the population is warm in winter. In the UK, there is some acknowledgement of this in the form of the winter fuel allowance for people over sixty-five, but still 17,000 die each year in England from causes attributable to fuel poverty.[64]

Some countries have developed special regulations relating to the duty of care for companies, which go beyond the traditional case law arising from negligence claims; for example, relating to product liability. The drive to decrease red tape, which we have discussed, and what is called the "blame culture" by recent UK governments has achieved one of its greatest successes in the Enterprise and Regulatory Reform Act (with its ironical acronym ERRA). The concepts of civil liability and duty of care are very closely related. The idea is that companies have a civil liability as a starting point – a bottom line – from which to study more-detailed issues covered by ALARP. This is contained in section 47 of the Health and Safety at Work Act 1974. However, ERRA removes this liability surreptitiously in section 69, so that breach of a duty imposed by health and safety law will no longer give rise to civil liability. Claimants now have to show negligence. This was a very retrograde move.

There is a strong case to be made that the UK Health and Social Care Act 2012 also weakened the duty of care of central government, by shifting accountability downstream to local authorities and the local Community Health Commissioners, whom I have mentioned previously. It was opposed vigorously as it undermined the origins of the NHS. The Secretary of State's overriding duty to provide a free and comprehensive health service was critically diluted with words such as "promote" rather than "provide", and by offloading the central duty of care to the local level. This has been described by opponents as the central government washing its hands of the NHS. The Secretary of State is now limited to a more passive, monitoring role with accountability hoovered up into a confusing network of chains of command. It is firmly believed on the left that this will open the door to a takeover by the corporations prowling around to pick up the most-lucrative contracts. There is a clause in the 2012 act that is ready and waiting to allow this: "The services provided as part of the health service in England must be free of charge except in so far as the making and recovery of charges is expressly provided for by or under any enactment, whenever passed." Although local accountability is, at face value, a good thing, and I shall champion the importance of community in the last chapter, the regressive nature of this new legislation seems cynical. It's as if, when the demand is for a duty of care at the centre, the centre says, "You want a duty of care? Okay, let me hand you some; I can't wait to get rid of it."

The concern that duty of care can be watered down by the actual physical outsourcing of manufacturing to far-off lands has led to calls for the duty of care to travel down the supply chains of the modern global economy.

On 24 April 2013, the Rana Plaza building in Bangladesh collapsed with a death toll of 1,134. Most of the deaths were of garment workers who had been ordered to come to work, despite cracks already having recently been found in the lower floors, which housed a bank that had already been evacuated. Many clothing companies operating in the West had been supplied by the factory, and this led to a major consumer-led campaign to improve accountability and conditions.[65]

In the UK, this disaster led to the Modern Slavery Act, and in France it led to the law on *le devoir de vigilance des entreprises donneuses d'ordre* (the duty of vigilance of parent companies). In the UK act, section 54 declares this:

> *[It] requires certain organisations to develop a slavery and human trafficking statement each year. The slavery and human trafficking statement should set out what steps organisations have taken to ensure modern slavery is not taking place in their business or supply chains.*

In the French act, companies over a certain size must do the following:

> *Establish and implement a diligence plan which should state the measures taken to identify and prevent the occurrence of human rights and environmental risks resulting from their activities, the activities of companies they control and the activities of sub-contractors and suppliers on whom they have a significant influence.*[66]

The ability of national and local government to pick and choose for which area it has a duty of care is explained neatly in the "Wrongs Act" of Victoria Province in Australia.[67] The perceived danger of an authority having once exercised a duty of care being required to continue it led to this new clause:

> *In a proceeding, the fact that a public authority exercises or decides to exercise a function does not of itself indicate that the authority is under a duty to exercise the function or that the function should be exercised in particular circumstances or in a particular way.*

One can imagine this in a relationship: "Just because I was nice to you yesterday does not mean I will be like that today." Case law is developing on the issue, including mention of budgets. Of course, there is tension between duty of care and resources. But our argument is that any case should, as for safety, be based on the notion of acceptance. The fact that the resources are not available to address a duty of care, new or old, should not mean that failure to fulfil a duty of care is acceptable. Furthermore, the areas that are addressed should not have to wait for disasters or campaigns by victims or by some senior body, such as the EU, finally agreeing to regulate in that area. If a duty of care is built into the system as a basic right, so that failures are unacceptable, then the kind of diffusion and watering down of the responsibilities of the government, as indicated previously, should happen less. The default position should be providing a duty of care.

Hansard provides revealing evidence of political hunger for what we might call a "general duty of care". Here is a valiant attempt by a member of the House of Lords to introduce the concept into banking:

> *Duty of care reflects that whole-culture approach: the underlying, underpinning approach that we expect our financial services to take, where the interests of the customer are at the centre. It is not that the financial services should not be able to make profits – of course, that is the business they are in – but it should never be at the expense of that central interest of the client or customer.*[68]

A private member's bill awaits its second reading.[69]

The area where duty of care is most strongly established by governments is towards its armed services. In a perhaps surprising burst of enlightenment, the UK government has established a firm duty of care – and, at the same time, admits that the funds are not always available – in the *Armed Forces Covenant*.[70] This remarkable document emphasises the triad of state, military personnel and society. It is refreshingly honest in laying down a general duty of care, while saying *at the same time* that there is not enough money to do everything the authorities would want to do. It calls on help from charities, the public service and communities, and it contains a remarkable promise to report every year on the progress made to honour its duty of care. The document resists using terms such as "proportionality" and "reasonably practicable", rather it uses the wonderful term "fairness". It shows the way for UK departments of state, ALBs and every regulator in the land to incorporate a duty of care in its terms of reference, with a requirement to report on such matters every year.

The *Armed Forces Covenant* has the courage to ask for special treatment of military personnel – or at the very least, not worse treatment – by the NHS. Rather than hide the possible ethical clashes, we should bring them into the open. In a period in which hospital waiting lists have been lengthening and there is evidence that an increasing number of patients are dying while on the lists, made worse by COVID-19, how long should a soldier have to wait for treatment? Please let us not have someone who survived a war in Afghanistan then die on a waiting list of a cash-starved NHS. The admirable duty of care now established for the military is in sharp contrast to that which is withering away in the NHS.

As someone who has actively been involved in the international peace movement in the past, it is natural for me to consider whether there is, or should be, some kind of generalised version of duty of care that extends across frontiers. We have seen that it does exist in areas such as modern slavery, in which duty of care extends down supply chains. It is a complex issue.

Duty of care, exercised rather than just debated, would lead naturally to intervention by the UN or a foreign power; for example, to prevent war crimes in the form of torture and the more extreme abuses. This is covered under both the "doctrine of the right of intervention" and "responsibility to protect".

These issues came to a head with the North Atlantic Treaty Organisation's (NATO's) intervention in Kosovo. An important report instigated by Kofi Annan, the UN Secretary General at the time, concludes:

> *Where a population is suffering serious harm, as a result of internal war, insurgency, repression or state failure, and the state in question is unwilling or unable to halt or avert it, the principle of non-intervention yields to the international responsibility to protect.*[71]

As mentioned previously, duty of care is heavily dependent on the concept of proximity, and this extends internationally in the sense that the highest duty rests with the state where the accident or abuse takes place. The difficulty arises when that duty of care is not exercised, then the more general duty is triggered.

Mahatma Gandhi's creed was not human rights so much as the duty of an individual to his fellow citizen. Duty, then, becomes part of being human. He recognised – along with others such as Bertrand Russell, who was active in the peace movement (Campaign for Nuclear Disarmament [CND] and the Committee of 100) – the importance of placing great emphasis on the personal; for example, on non-violence. Whether we call it virtue, spirituality, empathy or altruism, as the narrow definitions of duty of care are generalised and widened into an international responsibility to protect, without a personal commitment to our fellow individuals, no amount of law and agreement will really protect people from being sacrificed. We need political leaders and corporate executives with a strong personal and emotional commitment to a duty of care.

Do we *feel* a duty of care for those in small rubber dinghies in the English Channel, trying to reach our shores at this very moment? Or do we turn off the radio when we know that the British Navy has been called in to help?

7.

Life

"There is no wealth but life. Life, including all of its powers of love, joy and admiration."

John Ruskin[72]

A natural right is more or less the same as a fundamental human right, and it is intrinsic. Historically, it has been seen as a right given by God, and then, as the Enlightenment dispensed with God, declared to be fundamental, as explained eloquently by Alistaire MacIntyre.[73] I have noted that we have to be careful in adopting the concept of rights, because of the way they stalk the foundations of an extreme libertarian view adopted by Nozick and others in relation to property rights.

In ancient times, the sanctity of human life contained in the commandment "Thou shalt not kill" is qualified with a number of exceptions. It is okay to kill to protect the society in which you live, killing as punishment is allowed (unfortunately), and so on. Qualifications are also built into modern human rights law and laws related to warfare. As soon as the absolute right to life is qualified, it becomes clear that its strength depends on the relationship of the individual to the society, which Rousseau labelled the "social contract". In fact, this essay could be considered to be a health check on the state of the social contract. In a celebrated passage of his book on the subject, Rousseau says that our objective should be this:

> *To find a form of association which may defend and protect with the whole force of the community the person and property of every associate, and by means of which each, coalescing with all, may nevertheless obey only himself, and remain as free as before. Such is the fundamental problem of which the social contract furnishes the solution.*[74]

As explained, the social contract was rejuvenated by Rawls, who described a kind of ideal set-up in which one might come to an ideal social contract. The big snag is that governments do a lot of things for which the mechanisms needed to deal with externalities – the collateral damage – are not in place. Then we get angry citizens and expensive litigation. Part of the reason for this is that there is no real forum, other than Parliament and local councils, in which to thrash out the balance between natural rights and social good, or they are increasingly dominated by the problems of international relations, the global economy and powerful corporate interests.

At a certain moment in the life of John Ruskin, his anger at the appalling state of British society in which citizens were "crushed out in the slime of the street, crushed to dust amid the Rory of the wheel",[75] made him write the four essays collected together as *Unto This Last*. This is a carefully argued polemic against the economists and political thinkers of the age; that is, what used to be called "political economy". He championed openness, honesty and, above all, a richer valuation of human beings than the representation of them as crude, self-interested automata. In an elegant passage, he states this about economics:

> *Assuming, not that the human being has no skeleton, but that it is all skeleton, it founds an ossifiant theory of progress on this negation of a soul; and having shown the utmost that may be made of bones, and constructing a number of interesting geometrical figures with death's-head and humeri, successfully proves the inconvenience of the reappearance of the soul among these corpuscular structures. I do not deny the truth of this theory: I simply deny its applicability to the present phase of the world.*[76]

In another passage, he describes political economy as "the most cretinous, speechless, paralysing plague that has yet touched the brains of mankind."[77] Maybe that's a bit strong.

Ruskin had difficulty in getting the work published and – not surprisingly, given his strong language – received abuse back from the establishment. However, despite his voluminous and celebrated work on art, not least his championing of the painter Turner, he considered this small volume to be the best work he ever did. He stood his ground and garnered formidable supporters, notably Charles Dickens and, in the twentieth century, Mahatma Gandhi. Biographers say that reading Ruskin's essay changed Gandhi's life.[78]

Some of Ruskin's fiercest analysis is reserved for the notion of exchange. He stated that equations such as 1 QALY = £30,000; 1 life = £1,296,000; and 1 dead senior terrorist = 6 dead civilians are kinds of exchange. Not spending the £30,000 may cause one patient to lose a year of life and save the money to spend on other patients, but this is still an exchange. One of the problems with these kinds of exchanges, as Ruskin points out, is that they may be an exchange between an individual and a large institution. Whether that organisation is NICE or the US army, it has many advantages in terms of action and information. A free market of exchange, leading to equilibrium theories and the like in economics, requires information. More refined theories, such as the Nash equilibrium, make assumptions about "partial information", but my examples are almost as far as you can get from a free exchange. They are David-and-Goliath cases of the kind I discussed in connection with proportionality.

Thus, when we seek cases of sacrifice, we should think with a similar logic of situations encompassing the powerful with the knowledge versus the less powerful with less knowledge; and, of course, knowledge is power. Other examples we have seen are drug companies versus vaccination victims, corporations versus accident victims, and even ordinary investors versus insiders. The difficulty with the approach of utilitarianism and economics is that – despite counting people, counting money and even counting happiness – the human content that is life itself is at best oversimplified and at worst diminished. It is diminished at precisely the points of interface where hard choices are made, proportionality is ill-defined and the human being is most vulnerable. This represents a massive failure of imagination, plus a big dose of cowardice. Moreover, the failure of imagination is dangerous. Without the narratives of the victims, we may miss some causes and many of the effects. At the wild frontier of ethics, there are narratives that need to be told, otherwise the comprehension of causation itself is threatened.

In the desire to win the Nobel Memorial Prize in Economic Sciences or from a simple infatuation with mathematics, mathematical economics persists in trying to explain the behaviour of the human being as rational in a restricted sense, although there are movements away from the more rigid positions into the study of areas such as cognitive bias, altruism and happiness.

The word that is used by the young girl Sissy Jupe in Charles Dickens's *Hard Times* to capture the imagination in all its whimsical and poetic sense is "fancy". This beautiful word describes the day-dreaming free will at its most playful. Set against Sissy is Mr Thomas Gradgrind, a man of "facts and calculations". He preaches a crude but, for its time, fairly accurate version of utilitarianism, mixed with some rudimentary economics, and theories of supply and demand. The book should be compulsory reading for first-year economics students. Mr Gradgrind, with some skill, brings the arguments into the classroom. In his own words he is this:

> *A man of realities. A man of facts and calculations. A man who proceeds upon the principle that two and two are four, and nothing over, and who is not to be talked into allowing for anything over… With a rule and a pair of scales, and the multiplication table always in his pocket, sir, ready to weigh and measure any parcel of human nature, and tell you exactly what it comes to. It is a mere question of figures, a case of simple arithmetic.* [79]

An advantage of the medium of the novel is that the criticisms are brought to life via the relationship between characters and each personal story. As the economist Martha Nussbaum declares in her wonderful book:

> *… the normal shows, in its determination to see only what can enter into utilitarian calculation, the economic mind is blind: blinded to the quality and richness of the perceptible world; to*

the separateness of its people, to their depths, their hopes and loves and fears; blind to what it is like to live a human life and to try to inject it with human meaning.[80]

She carefully maps the ways in which emotions are criticised as not being rational, or not rational enough, to be the basis of a coherent methodology for human judgement and action. She goes on to answer a selection of these criticisms thus:

Utilitarianism takes its start from the fact of common suffering and is, at its best, motivated by the wish to relieve pain. So it is a very serious internal criticism of utilitarianism if it can be shown that the ways of reasoning in designated as "rational", by excluding emotion, deprive us of information we need if we are to have a fully rational response to the suffering of others.[81]

We have argued that a combination of a raw utilitarian approach, public policy epitomised by health economics, plus free-market libertarianism has hijacked much of public policy. It took a long time, but economics did eventually start to adapt to a world in which perfect markets are rare and people do not behave according to some conveniently restricted definitions of rationality. It started to take an interest in applied psychology. People can be optimistic or pessimistic, and demonstrate several other cognitive biases, which we can measure using cleverly constructed experiments. Another departure from the nineteenth-century version of economics is the cottage industry that has sprung up to study happiness, which tells us that there really is something more to it than the size of one's bank balance. The study of human behaviour has become big business. Teams of researchers and consultants offer analysis revealed by social networks, which are always on the lookout for new features of behaviour that may be exploited for marketing purposes, including (as I have mentioned already) in insurance. The holy grail of this activity is to find some kind of emergent phenomenon, which is not apparent at the level of the individual or a small sample of individuals. The term "thermo-economics" has been coined to cover the study of human behaviour using methods from the study of interacting particle systems.

In fact, it was already well known that the study of human behaviour is essential in safety-critical areas such aeronautics, both for pilots and air traffic control. The area is variously referred to as the study of human factors or human error. It is the acknowledgement of human fallibility arising from such studies that leads to demands for no-blame regimes. It is far better to really understand how mistakes arise in order to guard against them than to resort to expensive litigation.

Colleagues who work in the modelling of socio-technical systems may object to my following cheap summary of how models are calibrated: where parameters cannot be identified (estimated) directly or indirectly from data, we use guess values. We can improve this statement by replacing these guess values with expert judgement. The struggle between the objectivity of real data and the subjectivity of the human mind will always be with us. The Bayesian method of using data to update prior beliefs into posterior beliefs is probably the most successful currently. The elicitation of expert judgement is now a field in itself, and it extends not just to the values of attributes but to probabilities and correlations, both notoriously difficult to assess. But this is not the place to rehearse the cases for the different approaches. My point is that beliefs and judgements about systems involving human beings must require an understanding of human behaviour, and from there it is surely only a small step to say that human behaviour depends on human emotion. It is not good enough to say that human behaviour based on human emotion may be irrational because it clashes with some superimposed logic principles.

If the close connections between enlightened self-interest and the survival of the fittest can be linked forward to the utility-maximising rationality of neoclassical economics, then the study of altruism in evolutionary biology has also been reflected in studies of altruism in economics. Altruism also has a long history in moral philosophy. The broad question is whether altruism is really just a form of self-interest in disguise and can be divined with some clever change in the definition of individual utility or "fitness function", or whether it stems from some deep, emotional and moral concern for others, at least for those in the immediate family group or local community; that is, duty of care. What motivates human choice is an empirical question, and the conclusions that are derived from the dubious assumptions that economic motives dominate must be examined carefully. Several sub-areas will have to undergo severe revision, as motives other than economic gain, and especially altruistic ones, assume their appropriate place in the theory. My view is that any social or economic policy that effects individuals at the sharp end, or at the coalface, should be based not just on some kind of reductionist, rudimentary calculation but should, as fully as possible, include personal narratives.

The four parts of William Blake's 'I see the Four-fold Man' are reason, emotion, the senses and imagination. Roughly, his thesis is that only the living imagination can prevent reason dominating the emotions. His scheme was much admired by later writers, notably the poet W. B. Yeats. If we can extract it from its mystical landscape, while making allowance for the period in which he lived, then we can admire its brilliant vision. Blake's fear of the dominance of a mechanistic reason, which he calls "the Spectre", presaged many of the bleak pictures of rational modernity that stalk the twentieth century, such as in H. G. Wells's *War of the Worlds*, Ulrich Beck's *Risk Society*, Ronald Reagan's Star Wars programme and modern drone warfare. Blake's representation of the Spectre as a vampire bat seems to presage the modern drone, which strikes silently from the air.

Only imagination can save us. In the introduction, we stressed the importance of the imagination to escape from the straitjacket of utilitarianism and the primitive assumptions of modern economics. For Blake, imagination was the main life force, and one that combats his brutal Urizen of pure rationality. Without Blake's strong, mystical element, the American philosopher John Dewey also puts great weight on the imagination, which he sees as part of a more open approach to what he calls inquiry. He calls the "intelligent imagination" an instrument that looks beyond the details of empirical enquiry, towards hypotheses and situations that may be realisable; although this is not quite the unbounded imagination fuelled by thoughts of the infinite and transcendent, but it is very useful. We need Dewey's ideas if we are to claim that sacrifice is driven partly by a failure of imagination, which can lead to a failure of morality. In fact, Dewey is credited with the concept of the "moral imagination", which he places in a social context to underpin his open-society approach to education and democracy.[82]

There is enough food and water for everyone on earth. The difficulties are not those of volume but of access, allocation and what Amartya Sen calls "entitlement".[83] Scarcity is the quintessential challenge to the utilitarian view. The rot set in with Malthus:

> *A man who is born into a world already possessed, if he cannot get subsistence from his parents on whom he has a just demand,*

> *and if the society does not want his labour, has no claim of right*
> *to the smallest portion of food, and, in fact, has no business to*
> *be where he is. At nature's mighty feast there is no vacant cover*
> *for him.*[84]

His apocalyptic idea was that the expanding population, if not restricted in some way, would exhaust the earth's resources.

Malthus was writing after a long period of land enclosures in which wealthy landlords had gradually acquired great tracts of land, resulting in the massive displacement of the rural poor. His views are pernicious in three regards. First, by openly accepting the status quo, he is strong on defending property rights. Second, he says that the state should not be responsible for the poor. Third, he attributes the rapid increase in the population to the same poor, which is one of the greatest "blame the victim" stunts of all time. His views in some way permeate modern debates about neo-liberal versus welfare economics, and we can see why. Free-market economics, as I have said, needs scarcity, otherwise there is no subject. In particular, it requires a free market in labour, for which unemployment can lead to cheap labour, just as it did on the land in the England after the aforementioned enclosures, and continues to do worldwide now. Furthermore, it does not like a state that interferes with the market; for example, by introducing a minimum wage. Although here is the massive contradiction: free marketeers do not like the state interfering with market forces, but they are perfectly happy to accept the status quo, which is typically produced by the failure of the state to stop expropriation. So, in their terms, it is ideal for the state to accept or even promote structural inequalities while allowing the freedom for them to be accentuated by market forces. I am personally not against the market per se, but would claim that a market that starts with structural inequalities is not a free market, or at least it is not a fair market.

We can close the loop by arguing that the free market produces additional structural inequalities at the top end. A rich person can send their children to private school, which may lead to an educational advantage, or they can pass their property on to the next generation. Globalisation has spawned tax havens. It could be said that some versions of arbitrage (buying cheap and selling dear) are close to insider dealing, which is theft. All this increases the structural inequalities: today's new inequalities may be tomorrow's status quo. Some of the funds in off-shore accounts are being used to buy property in London. Part of this, we are told, is from money laundering from criminal activities. After all, land and property is a good thing to own, as the landlords in the enclosures and clearances knew. You can buy and sell it, and you can pass it on to your children. And they all – Malthus, Locke, Nozick et al. – shout that property rights are fundamental.

Talk of scarce resources in the public sector must be taken against this background. Every politician who uses the word "scarcity" should be reminded of what Malthus said. Every government department that bases policy on WTP should be reminded that this is the language of free-market economics. A tax regime that is friendly to the rich is friendly to the perpetration of structural inequalities that go back to the time of kings, queens, emperors, slavery and mass starvation. Politicians asking for a smaller state should know that there is no better way to declare that your position is essential political. If it is done indirectly as part of a financial package, as with Greece, it does not mean that the political and historical links are any weaker. But done by a leading politician, such as by George Osbourne, it places you firmly with Malthus, Von Mises, Hajek, Nozick,

Rothard and the right wing of the political spectrum: the extreme version of which is the "nightwatchman state".[85]

We have seen in Chapter 5 that accidents of birth or postcode lotteries, to which we might add many other structural inequalities, should not somehow be taken for granted. These are not like meteors from space, which can hit anyone, anywhere, and over which we have no control. The same is true of scarcity. Scarcities are not some permanent part of the structure or a *fait accompli*. I talk a lot in this essay about false formulae equating dollars to death, and about false comparisons under an umbrella of proportionality. These falsities are typically acted out on stages built by the powerful – the Goliaths; the stages on which the sacrifices are made.

We could say that if someone has been sacrificed for the public good, it is testament to the fact that that person has not been valued, but that is not technically correct in another sense. They *have* been valued, but as part of an exchange: a life is lost in exchange for the greater public good, where the public is now the previous public minus one. This chapter could have been titled "Value", but value is a concept with a dauntingly wide meaning. A value is often defined as anything that can be exchanged. However, value is varied: you can value highly your own life, and the people you love and respect. We all respect the brave nurses who put themselves at risk in the fight against the COVID-19 virus. WTP and WTA are all about value. Value is diverse and, most scholars will agree, cannot always be traded with money.

Here, I am not so interested in the values we may unconsciously attribute in our everyday choices, such as whether to have meat for dinner, or to go by car or train, although such a decision may have ethical implications; for example, in regard to climate change. What concerns me is the forced valuations imposed by scarcities or other administrative prerogatives, which lead to the abandonment of human rights. If there is not enough safety equipment for nurses, should they still go to work? These are the forced trade-offs between different value scales, limiting liberty, free will and, sometimes, life itself.

I have mentioned equivalence – the equals sign. The frontier between different value scales is fuzzy. It is well argued that scales often cannot be compared: love versus room size, or beauty versus wealth. However, in the kinds of situation in which people are sacrificed, decisions are hard *precisely because* the forced equivalence is unnatural. Article after article may be written debating whether, at the moment of choice, we are conducting a valuation, but there are not so many that suggest the number of such situations themselves should be made fewer. Society should value highly *not having to make* such value judgements.

One of the joys of writing in a research environment is that one idea or experiment points to others: they are predictive. This arises in conversation in statements such as "I wonder if there are other cases like that?". At that point, the scholarly approach is to see if the predictions are true; a less scholarly approach is simply to guess that there is such work, find a couple of references and leave it at that. I plead guilty to taking the latter approach sometimes.

So here is such a prediction: COVID-19 and probably climate change will, or have already, accelerated an ultra-utilitarian approach, as the difficult trade-offs between deaths and the economy build up. A test of this prediction would be the extent to which the trade-offs enter not serious democratic debate but the mathematics of the utilitarian approach: sophisticated equations containing – *at the same time* – money, GDP and human life. Before we look, we can guess that, buried inside the equations, there must be some kind of human-value parameters.

Here is an analogy. In physical equations, the quantities have units: typically mass (M), length (L) and time (T). (One can add other units such as charge.) Believing strongly that nature likes to balance the equations, scientists refer to equations as being dimensionally homogeneous, meaning that every term has the same exponents in M, L and T. Thus, if the equation is about energy, then every term will have units ML^2T^{-2}. Dimensional analysis is a method of creating dimensionless quantities, such as for viscosity. It may be hard to believe, but economists have developed economic theories in which money is added as a fundamental unit. This is not a joke.[86]

However, the following *is* a (sick) joke. Could it be that there are already equations being written in which M, L, T, £ and a new dimension of human life are incorporated? Well, we have already been given such a unity: Q for QALY. We can play dimensional analysis: cost-per-QALY has units $£Q^{-1}$. If T is the length of a life (or remaining life), then we have total cost per QALY as $T£Q^{-1}$. Given that there are rumours of the obese being denied certain forms of healthcare, we can add M for body weight, although we should correct for height: ML^{-1}. Plus, if health expenditure is less if B goes up (blaming the victim) then we divide the (allowed) cost per QALY by B to give our basic units of T, £, Q^{-1}, M^{-1}, L, etc.

Obviously, this is a joke that is not funny. We find increasingly, in our post-prediction searches, extensions of concepts such as WTP, ALARP and QALY. One is the value of a preventable fatality (VPF) – don't they just love acronyms and initialisms? Another is the concept of the J-value, which is an upper bound for what an organisation should spend on safety: "a safety scheme with a fractional J-value is acceptable. For example, if the J-value is 0.2, the scheme will yield a good safety benefit without using up too much resource."[87] Then, armed with new equations with their own definition of acceptability, these authors plan to contribute to areas such as the trade-offs between kick-starting the economy after, or in fact during, COVID-19.

The fear I have, and I have touched on this in reference to welfare functions and the like, is that the J-value or some other such mutant will become standardised into a universal definition of acceptable sacrifice, and that – rather than *duty of care* being written into all terms of reference of the regulators, as I suggest – what will appear will be the opposite: a duty *not* to spend too much; a duty to the taxpayer and the shareholder; a subservience to equals signs; inequality; and vast equations with units of time, money and human life. This would not represent a duty of care, but a duty to die,[88] or at least not to demand a level of care above the thresholds set by the government and spreading like COVID-19 itself into every hospital, care home and school. We have mentioned briefly the right to equality, but this should not be interpreted as being a right to an equal chance of being sacrificed. It should mean, rather, that we all have a right to be treated in a spirit of care, protection and rescue.

Sissy Jupe says it better: "I thought I couldn't know whether it was a prosperous nation or not, unless I knew who had got the money, and whether any of it was mine. But that had nothing to do with it. It was not in the figures at all."[89]

8.

Blaming the victim

"Where is the fairness, we ask, for the shift-worker, leaving home in the dark hours of the early morning, who looks up at the closed blinds of their next-door neighbour sleeping off a life on benefits."

George Osborne

In 2012, George Osborne, the then UK Chancellor of the Exchequer (finance minister) made a notorious speech to the faithful at the 2012 Conservative Party Conference; the above quotation is taken from that speech. The then Archbishop of Canterbury, the wonderful Rowan Williams, quickly pinned down this blame for the victim as "the quiet resurgence of the seductive language of the deserving and undeserving poor."

There is a large and connected body of work on victim blame, but one particular hypothesis stands out: the just-world hypothesis or just-world theory. In 1960, Dr Melvin Lerner carried out an experiment in which subjects were presented with female volunteer "victims" who were given electric shocks that were increased if they failed some tasks. The victims were also referred to using escalating derogative language and classified in a variety of ways. Some, the "martyrs", were described as suffering for the sake of the others, and some would get a reward and others no reward. There was also a "saved" category, when the torture could be stopped. The results show that the subjects tried to match the plight of the victims to the amount of punishment. They dished out the worst treatment to those they considered deserved it, namely the martyrs and the unrewarded victims. Conversely, the subject who was rewarded was the one for whom the reward was considered deserved, and the saved victim was innocent and rightly saved.[90]

The just-world argument goes like this. Assuming the world is inherently just, if a bad thing happens, something good has to balance that out in some way. Thus, if I am a politician and my policies seem unfair to an outsider, I must come up with a policy or judgement on the other side of the see-saw to keep it level. If I cut the benefits to people who are already poor, then I argue that they are lazy and good-for-nothing. I dip into my lexicon of disparaging terms: underserving, work-shy and scroungers. Their misdemeanours have to balance my cutbacks roughly, so as to leave the total amount of justice constant and my actions honourable. With a bit of luck, I will look fair to my supporters, who are the ones who will re-elect me. I can hold my head up high. Blaming the victim can just be a by-product of a built-in optimism that the world is just and that we must search for some kind of explanation for any calamity. On the other hand, it can be a deliberate attempt at self-justification. This would support the thesis, for which there is some evidence, that the just-world hypothesis is more endemic among the right wing of politics.[91]

Another explanation for the tendency to blame the victim can be worked up from cognitive dissonance when applied to decision-making. The idea is that, once a decision is made that has received criticism or may clash with other policies, there is an attempt to obtain or manufacture information in support of the decision in order to decrease the dissonance; i.e. the disparity. This may be familiar from everyday life. If the family decides to go camping in Brittany, and it rains a lot when they get there, then there may be an attempt to make the best of it by drawing special attention to the charm of the inhabitants, the wonderful food and the beautiful towns (all true). This is even if you may do better to go south to get the sun. One might add to this by vaguely insulting the South of France as being too hot and too unfriendly (not true). This becomes particularly pernicious when an argument *ad hominem* is used. This is when false prejudiced or irrelevant characteristics of an individual or group are used to add insult to injury.

John Offer gives a broad outline of the development of attitudes to the poor by separating the players into noetics and idealists.[92] Foremost among the first group is Herbert Spencer, whose philosophy is based on a social Darwinism, which is a belief in the survival of the fittest. Indeed, Spencer is credited with coining that phrase, and he argues against support from the state and supports charities or "private beneficiaries". According to Offer, the noetics had a strong influence on the Poor Law Amendment Act of 1834, which continued the ideas of there being both deserving and undeserving poor. The workhouse was to be the only way for the able-bodied to get relief, and local committees we set up to determine who was and who was not deserving. However, later reports, starting in 1834, began to take a more universal approach to welfare. The idealist is represented in the twentieth century by William Beveridge's universal themes of want, disease, ignorance and squalor, and the foundation of the British Welfare State, President Roosevelt's

New Deal, and the work of Richard Titmus and others in the post-WW2 consensus on welfare.

The story is a bit more complicated in that, even with the idealists, such as Beatrice and Sidney Webb (who were close friends of Spencer), there is an unpleasant, eugenic streak and a paternalistic notion that the state knows best. I have pointed out this danger before. Universal provision based on rights agreed by a democratic system is the idealist position, but where provision is cash limited, such a system has to decide who gets what. The danger then is the resurrection of the sanctimonious notions of the deserving and undeserving, and the use of them to justify austerity and discrimination against different groups. On the other hand, one can supposedly depersonalise the issues using complex rules related to quality of life, degree of disability, etc. I am not arguing that hard decisions do not have to be made, but there must be a better way than this either being via an anti-state ideology that writes off whole groups with the stroke of a pen, or a utilitarian robot spewing out decisions according to the latest algorithms of the health economists.

It could be argued that there is a direct link between the social Darwinism of Herbert Spencer and the views of Margaret Thatcher. Although, intellectually, this may be the case, it is hard to find any evidence of a direct link, such as Thatcher directly quoting Spencer. I am happy to be proved wrong. Better established as influencing Thatcher and her colleagues is the right-wing economist Friedrich Hajeck, as manifested in the neo-conservatives of the Chicago School of Economics. However, Spencer did resurface among a group opposed to the New Deal in the US. This was despite a demolition of his politics by Richard Hofstadter, who was the first to accuse Spencer directly of social Darwinism.[93]

In 1905, there was a notorious decision by the US Supreme Court when it adjudicated the landmark case of Lochner v. New York. The State of New York had enacted a law that limited the number of hours a baker could work to a maximum of ten hours per day and sixty hours per week. Rejecting New York's argument that the law was justified by the state's interest in protecting the health of its workers, the court decided by a five-to-four majority that such labour laws interfered with the "right and liberty of the individual to contract", a famous remark made by Justice Oliver Wendal Holmes, a remarkable thinker in his own right, in his minority report "The Fourteenth Amendment does not enact Mr Herbert Spencer's Social Statics".[94] The case was eventually overturned.

Anti-statism is closely related to the idea of "natural rights". I shall return later to ideas of rights, democracy and the social contract. Here, I want to point out that rights to life, liberty and property – which, as I have said already, are the hallmark of a libertarian approach – have also been used by anti-statists such as Spencer. At the boundary of rights, which is where one person's right may affect another's, a pure libertarian, such as Nozick, has to work hard to carry the argument through. Examples are where one person, under the right to property, monopolises some scarce resource or a medical treatment he has discovered. Nozick suggests that "A medical researcher who synthesizes a new substance that effectively treats a certain disease and who refuses to sell except on his own terms does not worsen the situation of others by depriving them of whatever he has appropriated."[95] We would rather say that the medical researcher sacrifices patients for his own profit. I believe these are a revival of Spencer's ideas. However, our main critique here is that they embodied the particular idea of the deserving and undeserving poor, and reversion to the notion of blaming the victim. If the lineage is accurate, then we ought to be able to find a modern libertarian who actual uses this terminology of deserving and undeserving poor. Michael Katz has fleshed this out in some detail.[96]

Some theories blame the ill for their illness. Patients who are instructed that they have unwittingly caused their disease are made to feel that they have somehow deserved it. Praising and denigrating the sacrificial victim is not just a feature of a world separated from ours by millennia, but is part of present-day rhetoric, culture and psychology. We see some kind of need by a certain breed of politician to separate subgroups of the population into two parts: the hard-working, who are deserving, and the others who are lazy and undeserving. Perhaps what we are talking about is a version of divide and rule. The politician can encourage the good half to take notice of, or even hate, the bad half (who are "sleeping off a life on benefits"), while the good workers trudge to their labours, through rain and snow.

The "blame the victim" culture is still being used today to distort health economics, perhaps with a hidden agenda of privatisation. I have pointed out before the central role of WTP in the foundation of health economics and safety, where panels selected from the public are used to help make decisions about resource allocation. But we must reserve our biggest criticism for a development in which the idea that certain groups, such as smokers and the obese, are less deserving of health resources. So, we have three groups now: the patients themselves, those who manage the resources and those who make value judgements about the patients.

In the UK, in order to save money, there are moves by some local health providers to deny obese patients routine operations. In a survey, more than one-third of NHS trusts are today considering rationing some types of surgery and other treatments.[97] Several have admitted they may impose eligibility rules, which could affect smokers as well as the overweight. Rationing has been resurrected. Here is how to play the blame game: (i) label those in the subgroup as good or bad, (ii) sacrifice the bad, and (iii) denigrate the bad in the eyes of the good. This is pure Malthusianism.

We are all good and bad at different times. At times, we are all lazy and not lazy, we are quiet and noisy, we love and hate (hopefully, more of the former), and we waste food and we hoard it. We may be too fat or too thin, and sometimes take risks and other times are careful. When we are young we drive too fast, and when we are old, other drivers toot their horns at us. To be otherwise would not to be human, but some politicians want to de-humanise half of the group, because it is easier to sacrifice non-humans. Ironically, they must not dehumanise them too much because then the good half would not think, as they are supposed to think, *There, but for the grace of God, go I* (and turn quickly to their diet books). A society in which panels are asked to help make decisions about individuals for the purposes of resource allocation is not so far removed from one in which individuals spy on each other, Stasi style, and then report the findings to the authorities.

In the expanding literature on responsibility in healthcare the term "deserving", as in "the deserving poor", has been replaced on the plus side by "merit", "meritarian" and on the minus side by "risk-taking behaviour", "reckless behaviour", and "imprudent behaviour". There is a whole vocabulary of blame, deserving some clever textual analysis using natural language processing or something; I might try that.

The theoretical basis of arguments in favour of denying some resources to people lacking merit is sometimes called "luck egalitarianism". The argument starts out well and suggests that inequalities that arise for reasons over which people have no control should be remedied by social and medical policy. I have used the term "structural inequalities" and do not like the word "luck", because of the false idea of some vast game of chance that it implies. The father figure of these ideas is Richard Dworkin, who sets up decisions about allocation as some kind of basic insurance policy that he claims any sensible person should subscribe to. However, the idea breaks down in its second level, namely that there should not be automatic cover for all those whose conditions can be said to be their own responsibility. It is not surprising that the ideas have come under considerable criticism, because it potentially drives a dangerous wedge between institutions, communities and even families: "My dad is too fat". Luck egalitarianism raises again the spectre of the deserving and the undeserving poor.[98] In these arguments and with a kind of puritanical glibness, the irresponsibility of the patient is often said to be manifested in one of the big three – smoking, obesity and drinking alcohol – and, if sometimes by analogy, gambling.

I like London, and we choose to live here, but it has a dangerous level of pollution in some areas, notably in the Aldwych by the London School of Economics. Under the Dworkin hypothetical insurance scheme, I should pay a higher premium or pay extra if I happen to develop asthma, bronchitis or chronic obstructive pulmonary disease (COPD), because, after all, I have only myself to blame for sacrificing my health for the joys of London. The same rules should apply to the brave medical staff in London hospitals.

Nevertheless, it is well known that obesity is related to social inequality. The poor tend to be more obese than the rich. It is also related to psychological issues such as depression. Any attempt to blame the patient for their obesity represents a wholly naïve approach to causation, and one that is deeply discriminatory and, by inference, class-based. Smoking is addictive, and some people try very hard to give up, but continue to fail. What is the causal pattern here? Is it that nicotine is very addictive, or do we include – as the blamers do – a lack of willpower or a kind of psychological inadequacy? If it has multiple causes, then which of the arrows in our causal network has the biggest weight? Surely, the common cause of poverty should be taken into account. There is an enormous counterfactual situation at play here. Maybe the cause is the failure of successive governments to get to grips with the power of the tobacco companies and the food processing industry? Once again, we see that moral decisions made at a political level may turn into some grizzly trade-offs at the frontier.

Theodor Adorno and others have blamed modernity itself for a type of dehumanisation that leads to sacrifice, using the Holocaust and anti-Semitism as the principal case.[99] Let's see if we can work through the argument. The enlightenment on which modern society is based brought with it modern science and the mechanistic view of nature: Blake's prediction. Two things happened. First, it was thought that, in regard to society, goodness could be described in terms of mathematical equations, just like in science. We have equations of economics, utilitarianism and evolution. Second, the modernists thought that this was enough. We could systematise the future and junk all those outdated theories of virtue, which had religious sources, after all. History was bunk, and we could all drive around in Model T Fords or Volkswagens, along broad highways lined with art deco factories modelled on a period of history when life was highly structured, such as ancient Egypt.

However, according to Adorno, things went wrong. The modernist spirit, with its strong lines and bright future, was hijacked by the totalitarianism of the Nazis and the Communists.

Their extreme version of modernism required conformity, and non-conformists were a challenge. Modernism destroyed us as human beings. You can see this in the brutal irony of Charlie Chaplin's wonderful film *Modern Times* and in Fritz Lang's *Metropolis*. So, a group that sticks to its long liberal, intellectual and humanist tradition, such as the Jewish community, presented a threat to the Nazis, and a threat to their totalitarian, modernist vision. Sacrifice becomes an attempt to dehumanise in the name of a modernist and conformist ideology.

Another reason for blaming the victim is that it offers a way of justifying the refusal to give compensation. There may be events – for example, being drunk and shouting – that contribute to dismissal in an employment tribunal. But there are many cases where it is used erroneously, such as in economic crime. There are published cases where banks have tried to blame the customer to avoid refunding for theft of stolen credit cards or hacked bank accounts. In the UK, many of these cases end up with the Financial Ombudsman who, thankfully, has strict rules that the customer has to have acted with gross negligence or fraudulently to be denied compensation. In law, something called "contributory negligence" will lessen or remove compensation.

The scholarship of sacrifice, from antiquity onwards, is very complex, partly because it is studied by both religious and non-religious anthropologists and historians. Documentaries and tourism have exposed sacrificial practices to a wider public; for example, the heartrending sacrifice of children in Peru. For Christians, the sacrifice of Jesus Christ carries profound symbolism and a central motif, which has been enriched by sacred architecture and painting for 2000 years.

The most popular explanation of the role of religious sacrifice is that it is used to appease a violent deity who is capable of inflicting terrible physical disasters: floods, droughts, earthquakes and so on. An interesting variant of this is a sacrifice to a predator as a strategy to give time for the majority to avoid being eaten alive. One sees similar in films when one brave, wounded soldier stays behind to allow the others time to escape.

Girard, a powerful critic of many of the more traditional explanations, offers yet another explanation.[100] He argues that sacrifice is used as an outlet for violent instincts, which might turn a tribe in on itself or foment battles between tribes. He succeeds in combining this with religious arguments by showing evidence that the sacrificial victim is in some way acting as a human who may actually be celebrated as an earthly representative of the deity, sometimes being deified themselves in the process. In Christianity, Jesus takes our sins upon himself, liberating us to be good. We might equally say that he's taking the violence upon himself so as to liberate us to be non-violent towards each other. There is some writing that uses such reasoning as a religious argument against capital punishment, which is a violent act after all.

This is a long and complicated story, but we can select one aspect and conjecture that its deep religious and anthropological thread may be traced to the present day. This is the need to blame the victim on the *lead up* to the sacrifice, as a way of justifying the violent act against him. However, in a secular world, there is no way to save the soul of the victim. This leads us to fall back on pious phrases about the public good, the war effort, the state of the national debt and the sanctity of the free market. We replace ancient gods with modern.

I have been trying to avoid writing a treatise giving a detailed analysis of the maximin principle from Rawls or others, but one point is evident: to exercise the maximin principle, a society has first to *find* the worst off. There should be no veil of ignorance when it comes to the raw facts. At the same time as blaming the victim for being undeserving in some broad Malthusian sense, using your favourite derogative term, you may want to hide them. First the act of dehumanisation, then the cover up. The reverse side of this is that if the victims have the audacity to be visible, to complain or even to sue, then that is the moment the invective reaches a crescendo.

Victims hide themselves out of shame or fear. The shame of poverty is a well-researched area that tells of the lengths to which families go to avoid being seen to be poor. It is hard. A child may try to help the parents be frugal at home, but then may have the shame of being less well kitted out at school than her schoolmates.[101] Only relatively recently have the victims of crime been brought into the judicial process after campaigns to continue to give them a bigger role. An example of fear is the fear of deportation that keeps many of the victims of modern slavery (an estimated 136,000 in the UK) out of sight. Anti-immigrant feelings may also help to keep them hidden.

It is a statistical irony that many victims of austerity and other kinds of public policy are hidden or camouflaged in the published figures of the government and regulatory bodies. There are many freedom of information requests to extract extra information or to seek clarity for existing data. The long waiting times for visits to the GP to have tests, or to get back test results prior to hospital appointments and treatments are one of the greatest complaints of the general public in the UK. Everyone who reads this will recognise the complaint that "I waited three weeks for an appointment with my GP and then only had ten minutes" (the current regulation). Although waiting-time information is available, it is better for certain conditions, such as cancer. Much is hidden. Detailed information about deaths while on waiting lists is a matter of guesswork. As stated in

Chapter 3, I am wary of the passive use of risk methods when they seem to hide the victims, but we should celebrate when they are used to *find* the victims as part of a progressive programme of action.

An extreme version of sacrifice by the state attributed by Paul Dumouchel is a distortion of the role of the state to protect its citizens (who are playing their proper part in the social contract) towards political violence.[102] Thus, we get genocide, ethnic cleansing and so on, which satisfies a need for enemies that the state finds internally rather than externally. It hides them by killing them, and while it is at it, it blames them too. If they try to hide, they are tracked down and killed to be truly hidden.

So we have to be careful. We need to know where the victims of our policies are hiding out of fear or shame, or where we have hidden them, sometimes in plain sight. But we are right to be suspicious. Is the visual surveillance of our everyday lives in London for our benefit? Is that sloping, hooded character outside St Pancras International Railway Station a homeless person selling *The Big Issue*, a potential pickpocket or worse? Are they one of us? Do we send in social services or the police? Does the automated surveillance robot classify people as okay, sick, poor or dangerous? When we find a victim, do we say – as Donald Trump seemed to imply – that they sort of shouldn't be there, and it's their fault if they are? Do the owners of the gleaming new buildings in London's Knowledge Hub around St Pancras surveil the people walking past, because they promised their insurance company to do so to avoid having to pay an insurance excess against terrorism?

9.

Drones

There is no more ambiguous and disturbing a euphemism than the term "collateral damage". Here is a definition from the US military:

> Unintentional or incidental injury or damage to persons or objects that would not be lawful military targets in the circumstances ruling at the time. Such damage is not unlawful so long as it is not excessive in light of the overall military advantage anticipated from the attack.[103]

Here people are not distinguished from objects, and the definition is soaked in a basin of qualification, which emphasises the legal and ignores the moral. One can be more precise by using the term "civilian casualties". This at least has a humanist feel to it, as with the term "patient" in the medical field. We crave the narratives; it might be you or me.

Not surprisingly, utilitarianism has raised its fists in the debate on civilian deaths in the guise of the just-war theory. We see their attempts to balance legitimate military objectives with civilian deaths using principles of proportionality. The value to the legitimate military objective of sending a missile to kill a senior combatant is to be weighed against the consequential death of civilians in the neighbourhood of the blast.

The Rome Statute in international humanitarian law does not legitimise military objectives when civilian injuries or deaths may occur. Direct attacks on civilians are forbidden in all circumstances. If we know that there would be excessive civilian deaths, the principle of proportionality would be breached automatically:

> *Rule 14. Launching an attack which may be expected to cause incidental loss of civilian life, injury to civilians, damage to civilian objects, or a combination thereof, which would be excessive in relation to the concrete and direct military advantage anticipated, is prohibited.*[104,105]

If something is expected, how can it also be incidental?

The Mark 82 500lb (226 kg) Moral Machine, which is the warhead of the GBU-12 guided bomb, has an effective casualty rate (50% casualties) radius of 60 metres, and a lethal blast radius (100% casualties) of 20 metres. It is very hard to get any official data, but campaigning groups have obtained aerial photographs showing extensive damage to buildings compatible with these figures and with the known effects of bomb blast pressure waves.[106]

There are a number of ways in which missile targeting can be wrong. To understand this, we must first appreciate the different levels of autonomy that these weapons have, the mix between human and non-human control, and the complexity of the mission. Mistakes can be human, and fall into the category of human factors, which is not too different from a mistake in air traffic control for civilian aircraft.

For me, one of the distressing phenomenon of drone warfare is that it has spawned a field of pseudo-academic activity, drawing on specialists in many quantitative areas. We have seen this elsewhere; for example, with the MIT Moral Machine. These might all be called the "arithmetic of sacrifice". We started with health economics and QALYs, then we continued with the risks of vaccination and compensation, the winners and losers of arbitrage, and the discriminatory technologies of personal insurance. These types of arithmetic have two things in common. First, they have both a scientific/technological side and an economic side: health with economics, fast computing with finance, and physical risk with insurance. Second, they make increasing use of sophisticated mathematical and statistical methods. Mathematics has been used in warfare from Galileo's work on ballistics to the modern era with the atomic theory of the nuclear bomb and automatic control theory in the development of missiles.

With drones, we now have a cocktail bar where we can mix the latest developments in decision theory, game theory and rational choice theory with signal processing, signature analysis, control theory and image processing, all combined to make cost-effective strikes on our enemy. As a professional statistician, I have first-hand experience of some of the methods used, or at least I know somebody who does. Here are some more initialisms: PCA (principal component analysis), PLS (partial least squares), ICA (independent component analysis), AI (artificial intelligence), ML (machine learning) and SS (source separation). A statistical approach would be to place confidence intervals around appropriate parameters and give a probability assessment of whether an enemy combatant has been found. And, of course, mixed into this cocktail will be a large dose (or shot perhaps?) of expert judgement. After all, the recognition of the enemy must include some judgement of human behaviour.

It may not be the case that all drone attacks are targeted at named individuals or groups of individuals. There is a new and more automatic type of attack called a "signature attack". The use of the word "signature" is interesting. Signature analysis has been used in a number of fields, and it can be considered to be a specialised branch of signal processing. It has been used, for example, in areas such as predictive maintenance; by running the laboratory tests or field trials on some mechanism, the signature of a fault or material wear of a certain kind can be learned. The mechanism can then be replaced or repaired before its failure leads to a serious incident. It has been used extensively; for example, in the online analysis of the vibration from aircraft engines. Similar methodologies are used to detect fraud in financial transactions: the signature of the fraudster. This type of analysis is becoming more sophisticated as a result of the big data revolution, because of the huge and multidimensional data streams that are increasingly available for analysis.

Because of military confidentiality, it is not possible to discover precisely what kinds of methodology are used in a signature attack, but we can make a shrewd guess. Images of various kinds are analysed to trawl for the signature of an enemy combatant or group. This signature would show up as a departure from some kind of normal (a sociologist might use the term "normative") human behaviour. Following the detection of such a signature, a decision would then be taken as whether to attack or not.

One among many worrying features is that signature analysis has a component of learning. That is to say, one needs to feed back information in order to calibrate and improve the underlying models. With an aircraft engine, the physical wear would be compared with the predicted wear, as measured in laboratory testing, in order to improve or calibrate the model.

This requirement makes it likely that signature-attack models are designed to learn whether, at the time of the attack, there was information about victims: whether they were indeed combatants or non-combatant civilians. In essence, then, a drone attack is not just a military action, it is also a grim experiment to calibrate advanced mathematical and statistical models. The balance between exploitation and exploration is at the foundation of modelling in noisy environments. In this case, the exploitation is killing people, but if the model is not properly calibrated (exploration), the wrong people may be killed.

The engineering side of drone warfare is captured under several acronyms/initialisms of which the most fashionable is MEMS: micro-electromechanical systems. These combine mechatronic (electro-mechanical) functionality with AI, all embedded in layers of silicon semiconductor chips. The Defense Advanced Research Projects Agency (DARPA) itself boasts about its plans:

> *Areas targeted for heightened attention and investment by DARPA informed the development of many of the top technologies singled out by the Department of Defense's Under Secretary for Research and Engineering for urgent attention and modernization. These include hypersonics, with applications for offense and defense; microelectronics; and artificial intelligence/ machine learning.*[107]

The systems are flexible, can adapt to changing environments, and contain several of the ingredients in my aforementioned cocktail, such as sensing and control. With such systems, drones become flying robots that can identify targets and make strikes. As the weapons become more autonomous, the complexity of the relationship between the human-in-the-loop (or the pilot) may lead to more human error, not less. There is evidence that, since the introduction of drones, the proportion and number of civilian casualties has increased, although this is strongly denied by the military.

The anxiety of civilian populations about being hit by drones must be multiplied by a thousand if the drone can strike with little or no warning, the first drone was the German V1 flying bomb in WW2, nicknamed the "doodlebug" or "buzz bomb" because of the distinctive motorcycle-like sound of its engines, before it cut out, dropped silently to the ground or near the ground, and exploded. We know all this, not just from history books but because our parents and grandparents told us so (in this case backed up by the British Broadcasting Corporation's [BBC's] wonderful archive).[108] Numerous harrowing accounts can be found of both the physical effects and the psychological effects of drones on civilians. This is a prime example of the need to capture the narrative of the victims, which is often almost too agonising to absorb. As if the death and maiming of civilians were not enough, the long-term effect on the community and political structures is incalculable, as is the long-term effect on international relations and the quest for that elusive peace. The huge demonstrations against the drone attacks in Pakistan and the declaration by individuals that it was drone attacks in particular that drove them to militancy should change minds in Washington DC and London.

Gregoire Chamayou, in his remarkable book *Drone Theory*, etches the difference between peacetime and wartime in terms of the nature of decision-making.[109] In peacetime, part of the social contract is that the state will protect the citizen, whereas in wartime, the situation is reversed. The citizens are called upon to protect the state, and that may involve their sacrifice. We can even think of some kind of philosophical regress: the citizen protects the state so that the state survives, in order to protect the citizen, and so on. Our earlier protest that it is not in the public good to sacrifice someone for the public good becomes an even bigger contradiction in wartime. In fact, this is precisely the source of my objection to the poisonous ethics of war seeping into civilian life.

An all-powerful sovereign can continue the regress, only impeded by revolution or defeat, whereas a democracy can decide to go to war only in extreme circumstances. It may decide not to go to war for many reasons, such as the economic cost, the danger of escalation or a tradition of passivity and neutrality, but the biggest reason may simply be a refusal to sacrifice its citizens for a cause that it thinks does not merit the sacrifice.

Think how this equation changes when war can be conducted remotely with no sacrifice of one's own combatants. Think also of how arguments that the accuracy of the drone strike leads to less collateral damage can be used to improve the moral balance. Unimpeded by some of the negative aspects of war, those arguments that are typically discussed in the debates in the House of Commons are that an administration can create a secret war room from which it can target anyone it wants, anywhere in the world, and only reporting back to the debating chamber when it has a "success". Ironically, with no men and women being sent to die in foreign war zones, there may be no mass anti-war movements, in the style of the anti-Vietnam war and anti-Iraq war movements.

Chamayou reminds us that, with access to combatants across the British Empire, Britain was better able to conduct wars with lower risk to its citizens. He quotes Hobbes – "each man is bound by nature, as much in him lieth, to protect in war, the authority, by which he is himself protected in time of peace" – and he doubts whether this relationship is any more reciprocal.[110]

One of the founding principles of the just-war theory is the "double effect doctrine".[111] There are roughly four parts to the doctrine. The first is to do with intention: an act of war must only be carried out by a legitimate authority. Second, it must be justified by good intentions. The third is the acknowledgement that there may be a double effect: on both the enemy combatants and on the civilians, with the former being intended and the latter not being intended. The fourth is the proportionality thesis: the intended benefit of the attack, in terms of the destruction to the enemy, must outweigh the effects on civilians in some way.

This morally bankrupt cost-benefit analysis is an extreme example of the David-and-Goliath imbalances that we have seen in civilian life. Always, there is a central concern (killing a terrorist, making a profit or protecting against an infectious disease) and an externality, which is, as I have said before, seen as a secondary effect compared to the well-defined exchange taking place. Compare the word "unintended" in the standard definition of an externality, which is something like: an unintended action caused by an economic agent that directly influences the utility of another agent, with the famous definition of Thomas Aquinas, father of the double effect, which is "Nothing hinders one act from having two effects, only one of which is intended, while the other is beside the intention."[112]

In summary, all of these terms – double effect, collateral damage, side effects and negative externalities – are the language of sacrifice. It is a language that can be linked to theories developed in mediaeval times to justify wars. This is also the source of the dubious term "proportional". My fear is that this language, which began in the study of war, should spread into peacetime, as it is language that is unjustifiable even in wartime. The antidote I put forward is that of acceptability. Once the double effect and the concept of proportionality are accepted as inevitable, then it opens the way for every kind of iniquity and inequity. These doctrines are disingenuous in the sense that they are a deliberate attempt by the victor to monopolise the moral capital. They are an elaboration of the idea that God is on our side. The victims of the "unintended" consequences are awarded a minor role, like the innocent citizens in some mediaeval siege.

At this point, we could enter into the philosophical debates about consequentialism: is it the consequences that matter or the virtue (or otherwise) of the instigator? The argument in the last paragraph is consequentialist, because we are judging the effect on the victims, which is the secondary effect. We do not trust the pious self-justifications of the victor. My difficulty with the consequentialist argument is that it permits calculation, and a weighing up of benefits and disbenefits to give an overall goodness tally. Such calculations in which lives are traded off against lives, or lives are traded off against money, are utilitarian calculations. These fake proportionality-based arguments are typically cooked up by the victor.

If there are two effects, the primary (A) and the secondary (B), then we should not be measuring the consequences by the net value $C = A - B$, such that if C is positive, we are allowed to go ahead and sacrifice B. We have abhorred the PTO. It is much better to make C zero by *making both A and B zero*: don't go to war at all if you are going to kill civilians. That, in our terms, should be the acceptable default position – the point from which the discussion should start. No one should be killed on a building site, vaccines should not have side effects, we should not have child malnutrition and no old people should die of hyperthermia. We should start with $A = 0$.

Finally, it seems that, at this moment, there is an infatuation with DARPA and the use of advanced technology in warfare in the present UK Cabinet Office. It is frightening to think that, whereas some of us involved in the development of technology and its mathematical handmaiden have always been wary of its use in warfare and the possibility of a never-ending arms race, there are powerful neophytes who have never been on an anti-war or peace march, are not old enough to hear their grandfathers talk about going over the top in World War I (WW1) or living through the blitz in WW2, and who embrace drones with prurient fervour.[113]

Let us remember what C.P. Snow said in his critique of Churchill's "mad professor" Linderman, the one who pressured Churchill for the aerial bombing of German civilians:

> *It doesn't matter how confident he is; if he is confident because of the euphoria of gadgets, he is doubly dangerous. The point is, anyone who is drunk with gadgets is a menace. Any choice he makes – particularly if it involves comparisons with other countries – is much more likely to be wrong than right, the more he is going to mislead his own country.*[114]

10.

Free 'n' frank

"Democracies die behind closed doors… When government begins closing doors, it selectively controls information rightfully belonging to the people. Selective information is misinformation."[115]

Judge Daynon Keith

The right to freedom of information has been growing in political importance at about the same rate as governments have done their best to impede its progress. The "insufficient resources to investigate" lament of regulators is mirrored in the complaints from the UK government about the cost of meeting requests for information. Similarly, the "Not my job, guv" from regulators is mirrored by the many exemptions from the Freedom of Information Act.

Here is section 36 (2)(b) of the UK Freedom of Information Act: "The exception applies to any request which would, or would be likely to, inhibit (i) the free and frank provision of advice, or (ii) the free and frank exchange of views for the purposes of deliberation."[116]

Although there is a public interest appeal, what a nice summary this is of the term "behind closed doors". And what a good name for a pub "The Free 'n' Frank" would be (maybe a hole-in-the-wall bar near the Houses of Parliament), or it would make a great name for a pair of bowler-hatted civil servants, like the Thompson twins in the *Tintin* cartoons.

It is, or should be, a basic element of the democratic process that the public have access to information on which the decisions are made by the government. This should include any background policy, objectives, and – in principle – any mathematical, scientific or social theory being used. But there is something more. If the decisions are made behind closed doors, then – even if we see all the background information and the final decision – we will miss gaining any insight into how the decisions are actually formulated in The Free 'n' Frank wine bar. What exactly is the special truth-telling called "frankness" that goes beyond what a reasonable person, or perhaps a university research group, might articulate in proposing a solution? If it's national security, then that's okay. But if it concerns some corporate vested interest, some political embarrassment or, above all, the needs of some community, then we have a right to know.

The list of wrong decisions taken by the UK government since WW2 surely disqualifies it from imagining that the best decisions are taken in secret. It should be part of resolving forced choices that we discover their source. We can suspect that many requests for information under the Freedom of Information Act stem from this aim, and that many of the often patronising refusals stem from the kind of embarrassment we have referred to previously as the cowardice of politicians. In a magnificent chapter entitled "A deficit of deliberation" in their book *The Blunders of Our Governments*, Anthony King and Ivor

Crewe opine that "The notion that British governments have a special gift for decisiveness and the taking of tough decisions is largely a myth – a myth propagated by governments themselves. In truth they prevaricate, procrastinate and defer as often as they decide."[117]

In his book *The History Thieves*, Ian Cobain gives a deeply depressing portrait of a British establishment that has hardly deviated from the worship of secrecy since the launch of the Official Secrets Act in 1922. He describes in detail how it has been used to hide dubious trials and destroy hundreds of important historical documents, and how there are still secret vaults around the country with material relating to the dark days of the British Empire.[118] The UK government has only just begun to declassify over a million documents at Hanslope Park, including many records related to slavery.

The other side to secrecy worship is the continuing *obstruction* to freedom of information, first in the watering down with exemptions in the Freedom of Information Act itself, and its delayed introduction, but also in its day-to-day workings. Unfortunately, we now have worse: a committee of inquiry on the Freedom of Information Act has reported recommendations that threaten to degrade even further the "public interest" appeal which is available in section 35 of the Freedom of Information Act, with its forty-four exemptions:

> *The existence of a safe, internal, deliberative space allows for frank discussions and advice, and for the consideration of the full range of options, including some which might, after deliberation, be deemed to be unacceptable, and for these to be criticised and challenged. It is important that ministers and officials should not feel discouraged or impeded from setting out deliberative material in written form during a deliberative*

> *process. If these internal discussions are to be made public soon after a decision is taken, then this undermines the entire principle of a safe space. In the context of policy decisions, this interpretation would mean that unless there are additional factors that render pre-decisional material sensitive, advice from officials and records of frank discussions of options would be immediately releasable once a decision is taken. We do not see how participants can feel confident to engage in frank and imaginative deliberations when they know that these deliberations could be made public the moment that a decision is taken. It is no response to this concern to say that in most cases people do not make requests under the Act for this information: the fact is that they could, and officials and ministers are not to know in which cases requests will be made.*[119]

Oh dear! "Frank" is now to be housed in a "safe space", which is called a "principle". And lo and behold, we have the new allegorical pair on the block – "Frank" and "Imaginative" – and their sister "Deliberation". Surrounded by the pillars of the establishment, our rulers are to have a safe garden of earthly delights from which the gaze of the public is excluded, with not even a little window through which we can kibitz on their hidden pleasures. In their secret garden, they can become poets of the imagination, maybe even geniuses. Maybe Jerusalem is to be "builded" in the Cabinet Office.

Nevertheless, it is not the sheer level of pompous elitism that is disturbing in the prior extract, it is the commandeering of the word "deliberation". Even a cursory reading of political theory would tell the commissioners of this report that the word "deliberation" is used mostly today in the context of "deliberative democracy" as opposed to the safe confines of the jury room or cabinet. As for the "safe space", let us assume that they mean it to be the "defensible" of architecture, and thus a space safe for children to play, not the modern and highly controversial place for particular groups to talk, with its controversial implications for freedom of speech.

We could devote much reading time to political writing that seeks to promote the privileged position of elected representatives to lead without too much day-to-day interference from the electorate. It is clear from the continuous demand by the government for the accountability of the public sector that at least accountability upwards is here to stay. But accountability downwards is less secure, and freedom of information should be a critical element in achieving it. We do not want governments to take actions that they would not have taken had we known why they were taking them, and one reason they would not have taken them is because a certain vocal subgroup was disadvantaged. This is a version of the Broome paradox: if the risk for a particular subgroup is increased, the government may think, *Either we don't do it, or if we do it, let's not tell the subgroup that they are the victims.* This means even more that we have to know what the governments are doing, and why they want to act independently and without full disclosure. Their authority to rule should not include the authority to hide information from us, an extreme version of which is when a government hides information deliberately from the public because they know it will damage their chance of re-election. To sign off on the social contract, we need freedom of information, just as with any contract. Of course, the contract will be imperfect in that not every eventuality can be foreseen, but to withhold important facts, including policy intentions, is anti-democratic.

11.

The critical path to 2050

This essay has been too long in gestation; so long, in fact, that events seems to be rushing past as if some crazy Dickensian schoolmaster was looking to distribute yet more exam papers to tired school children. But there is one exam we all have to sit, even though the coronavirus is trying to make us cancel the exam. Let us see if anything that we have said in previous chapters can possibly help us get to that 2050 target of zero net carbon. The impacts of climate change are already being felt, and the young have taken up the cause of climate change with the same determination that other generations and communities have championed other causes, such as peace, nuclear disarmament and #MeToo.

From a professional point of view, the problems of designing and following what the EU euphemistically calls the 2050 Road Map[120] should be like any large-scale project, which requires a plan and very good project management. Critical as we shall be about the plethora of new, tall buildings in London, we can secretly admire the speed and efficiency with which they are designed and constructed. They use a portfolio of computer-aided methods: cost accounting, risk management and critical-path programming. On asking an insider about one company's methods, I received the reply to the effect that everything is designed and costed down to the last screw.

It seems, however, that no government, and certainly not the EU, yet has a critical path to get us to net zero carbon by 2050 or preferably even sooner. What we have somewhere are lists of possible new markets, measures, impact assessments and scenarios that may or may not lead to rules and directives, and for the adoption of which we do not yet have the necessary collaboration between states. The recent UK election provided a nice contrast between a party with interventionist intentions (Labour) and the victors (the Conservatives), with some declared intentions but a history of *laissez faire* in economics and austerity in public expenditure. Neither really seemed to have grasped at that stage the urgency of climate change. There can be no greater public good than saving the planet. The natural impulse is to shout loudly, "We should all pull together!"; as our great grandparents would ask, "Don't you know there is a war on?"

Here are some signposts on the critical path: (i) change corporate governance to include public-good clauses, so they can be instructed to decrease carbon; (ii) get rid of all domestic gas boilers; (iii) invest massively in retrofitting old buildings with new insulation projects; (iv) offer tax incentives and cheaper electricity for heat pumps, solar panels, etc.; (v) invest in all forms of renewable energy: wind, hydro, wave, biomass, etc.; (vi) implement carbon capture; (vii) mandate all cars to be electric or hydrogen; (viii) use hydrogen for fuel where feasible; (ix) subsidise public transport; (x) provide better storage of electricity and heat; and many more, including my favourite, (xi) make sure the key regulators have not been "captured" by those being regulated. We know the measures, but we don't yet know the when and where, and certainly do not yet show the political will to carry them all out before it is too late.

The prevailing view is that we cannot get there without intervention. The market will not deliver, in the same way that it did not reduce inequality under globalisation when some got richer – much richer – but only a minority, and it also accelerated climate change. Political will implies, by definition, that governments must act and must intervene for the public good. But irreversible climate change has been gathering pace at the same time as other political changes have been taking place. Here is the problem: if dealing with climate change requires a massive level of intervention by governments, we are likely to see a reaction against the increased centralisation that intervention will entail. The UK has just rejected control from Brussels, and surveys show that the EU institutions are not universally popular. In Catalonia, the independence movement has been supressed. Scotland is bidding for independence.

At every staging post along the road to 2050, there will be trade-offs of the kind that this essay urges us to look for, to highlight, to discuss, to eliminate if possible and to compensate for when that's impossible. The danger is simply stated. Just as civil liberties are constrained in wartime, so in peacetime the "war" against climate change may have the same effect.

My view is that it will be impossible to reach the climate targets without a pact, or a social contract, between governments and the people, and governments and communities. It may be that, on many other matters, governments can sneak through some policies on the domestic front – based on outdated, utilitarian philosophies – and outsource ethical decisions to unelected, arms' length agencies, but this will not work for climate change. A weak version of this realisation was voiced in a recent interview:

> We are simply told that a government has made a decision among various policy options and that's it. But I think there is, as you say, because of the backlash, going to be a much greater premium on more detailed explanations of why decisions have been taken.[121]

Backlash is an understatement. If the Gilets Jaunes in France can be stimulated to riot because of a fuel price rise, what may happen when carbon-producing utilities are closed down; the internal combustion engine is banned; draughty, old buildings are pulled down; communities are moved because of sea-water rises; there are more forest fires and desertification; and beef and lamb are no longer on the menu?

All work on climate change tells us that the greatest *impact* (a key word) will fall on the poorest.[122] A breach of duty of care by the defendant is one of the reasons that one may make a successful claim for damages, although in many countries, including the UK, it is – as explained – hard to sue the government or a public authority, even if you can bear the cost. With climate change, there is a particularly difficult technical issue when it comes to trying to sue governments or to get payouts on insurance. This is the issue of *attribution*: what fraction of a catastrophe, such as a forest fire, can be attributed to climate change?[123] This is the first step in determining liability. The issue is essentially the same as for vaccination and other cases where there is a special event: it is the difficulty of proving causation. Of course, the requirements in civil cases may be on the balance of probability rather than something being beyond reasonable doubt, as in a criminal case. Nonetheless, we need to know the cause.

The issue is sometimes called the problem of "singular causation", and it is already the subject of debate within climate science. There has been incredible effort in climate modelling, which predicts what will happen to the temperatures if we do or do not reduce carbon emissions. Most of these models use the scientific method: a combination of deduction and induction, physical laws, and data from historical weather reports combined with modern satellite imaging, and many other new measurement methods. However, the argument goes that these predictions are now institutionalised, and great care is taken not to cry wolf and be over-alarmist. A recent discussion says this:

> *Climate scientists sometimes analyse "extreme events", like storms, floods, or droughts, and try to determine whether such extreme events were partially caused by climate change or not. The standard method for doing this analysis is called the "risk-based" method. It carries the risk of underestimating the role of global climate change in extreme events and missing connections that are really there.*[124]

So, along comes a really serious event, such as the recent Australian and Californian forest fires. The question is whether they fit into the normal pattern of extreme events, and if not, what caused it. Can we prove causation from the *singular* event itself? Such a method has been named the "storyline approach". The idea is similar in spirit to my requests earlier in this essay, that we should listen to the narratives of the mother with the vaccinated child, or those of the elderly patient denied the new drug. The solution, or at least a suggested course of action, is to investigate the event in great detail to look at the conditions under which the event took place. It may then be clear that those conditions, which form a kind of causal envelope, can be influenced by climate change. We don't have time to wait around to have a nice, big sample of forest fires so that we can work out some kind of confidence interval.

This kind of singular causation is available to us on an everyday basis. It is sometimes called "inference to best explanation". Why did our visitor not arrive? Is she ill? Did she miss her train? The answer for which could be that, well, she looked fine yesterday, and she would have phoned or texted if the train had been delayed. It is a forensic-style approach that requires experience, yes, but it is also required when it is a rare event (she is always very punctual). Imagination is needed: maybe she accidently got on the wrong train?

Hence, from the general propositions in this essay, we can ask the question that a colleague asked me recently: so what is your angle on climate change? They may equally have asked what my angle is on the climate emergency. For this, we need to go back to our opening paragraph and ponder whether, because it could be said that we are engaged in war against climate change, we should be on a wartime footing. If we say this, then we are in danger of resurrecting wartime ethics, just when we have spent our effort opposing exactly that. Note also a creeping respect, even jealousy, that countries such as China – where the government is able to intervene (some say like a good Keynesian) as much as it wants – are in a strong position to make a big impact. The argument might also say that we need strongman governments to fight climate change, just as we needed strongman governments to defeat the Nazis.

My personal fear is that the *force majeure* of climate change may allow in all the naïve utilitarian principles that we have been arguing against; it could open the Pandora's box of shoddy ethics. Individuals and communities will be sacrificed for the (global) common good, and there will be new talk of proportionality and VSL. Health economists will charge into the area of climate change armed with their QALYs. Politicians will tell us there have to be winners and losers. Experts will hide behind pre-event calculations of risk, and the risks will be traded in some vast new gambling halls, which are full of economists promoting new market-based solutions and awarding prizes for new theorems in thermo-economics. I am not unique in having this fear. It is well captured under the heading of "climate change and human rights":

> While the failure to report on the linkages between human rights and climate change is not itself a violation of human rights obligations, it does suggest that many countries are not thinking about these obligations when formulating climate change plans and policies. It also makes it more difficult for the international community to assess what countries are doing to address the human rights implications of climate change.[125]

So the requested angle is the following: every trade-off and every hard (forced) choice along the road to 2050 must be brought into the open. It must be the subject of discussion and of deliberative democracy. There is an overriding reason why this is essential: we will not get to the zero-net-carbon target without taking a willing public along for the ride. At the moment, the campaigning part of the public is taking the lead; it is in the driving seat. To abuse the metaphor: if the radical environmental movement and the progressive governments manage to get into the driving seat of the global charabanc, it will not look good if, on the road to safety, thousands are left to perish along the roadside.

12.

The democratic deficit

Politicians talk and we respond – with our votes. But the truth is quite other. Most people don't feel as though they are part of any conversation of significance. They are told what to think and how to think. They are made to feel inadequate as soon as issues of detail are engaged; and as for general objectives, they are encouraged to believe that these have long since been determined.

Tony Judt[126]

We need to take stock. I started with a critique of a rule-based, utilitarian approach to the rationing of healthcare in the UK. I find offensive the equating of people's lives to money in the arithmetic of the QALY, and its counterparts in health and safety, and the spurious sophistication of the social welfare function. The trading off of people's lives is acting directly against basic human rights, as enshrined in laws and treaties. We do not have the right to trade lives. In addition, I do not accept the scarcities that are predicated on ideological stances, which include refusals to adequately tax the wealthy and predilections for a small state, which is an ideology that can be found even in the health directives containing reference to taxpayers and strange economic terminology such as "disinvestment". At worst, these views are combined with a tendency to blame the victim, which can be traced back to Malthus and the social Darwinism of Herbert Spencer. Tony Judt says:

> ... there can be no doubt of that what passes for justification of the vast and growing wealth gap in the modern Britain derives directly from the apologetics for limited regulation, minimal interference and the virtues of the private sector to which the Austrian economic writing contributed in so directly.[127]

However, we have discovered another tradition that celebrates human life and refuses to equate cash and life in some mathematically and administratively convenient and naïve way. This tradition can be traced through Rousseau, Blake, Payne, Ruskin, Dewey, Roosevelt and Beveridge. It survived two world wars and broadside attacks from right-wing Austrian economists and their Chicago henchmen to emerge into the Welfare State and the UK/Nordic model of social democracy.

The risks discussed in this essay in relation to sacrifices made by ordinary people are manifestations of the kind of risk inherent in what Ulrich Beck calls "the risk society".[128] Both he and Anthony Giddens[129] tell us that, on the one hand, the onward march and expansion of modernity carry forward all the old risks and many new ones, and on the other, we may have the capacity to deal with these risks by using the right technology and the right institutions. The biggest risks are from climate change and globalisation. Giddens is an advocate of the public–private partnership and was the architect of the "third way", which was adopted by the New Labour government of Tony Blair. In many ways, this was an optimistic utopian vision, but one now shattered by the world financial crisis, Brexit, COVID-19 and climate change. The cosy relationship between the corporations and the government led to dangerous soft-touch regulation. In opposition to the views of Beck, Giddens and others is the idea that we are already in postmodernity, because the 68er student "revolutions" had already challenged the old order. Even back then, the mirror of modernity was shattered into new and inclusive types of social interaction, which are manifested today in movements such as #MeToo and Black Lives Matter.

Architecture is a good way to track attitudes to modernity and postmodernism, with the latter term being reserved for a derivative anything-goes approach to culture. It is interesting that, after WW2, a humanist modernism was promoted by architects such as Alvar Alto in Finland and Bertholt Lubetkin in Britain. This is a person-centric style summarised by Lubetkin's declaration that "nothing is too good for ordinary people".[130] But rather than achieving this vision, in London, large, prestigious buildings designed by "starchitects" dominate the city, along with only a small (often zero) percentage of social housing.[131] Architectural reviews use words such as "exhilarating", "exciting" and "signature".

In London, there are huge forces at work. Many of the large, prestigious architectural projects are funded by inward investment, and in many cases, the ownership is obscure and offshore, and it is conjectured commonly that these investments are for tax-avoidance or money-laundering reasons. This property development is also distorting the housing market. Those who are not already established home owners cannot afford to get on the housing ladder. Local authorities struggle to provide social housing and to force big developers to meet their promises on the scant amount of social housing that the new buildings provide. The public sector workers, cleaners and carers who keep the city running are squeezed out, and homeless families are literally moved out of London, away from their communities. The single homeless live on the streets. Just north of the London School of Economics, in Lincoln's Inn Fields, a mobile soup kitchen is set up every day.

Meanwhile, the EU's Smart Cities programme[132] puts forward a utopian view of cities that are safe, and with clean air and water, easy-to-use public transport, efficient services, green areas and so on, which are all integrated with high-tech communications. Is the Smart Cities programme simply another manifestation, built on modernist technology – the city of Dan Dare of the *Eagle* comic and of Harold Wilson's the "white heat of technology" – which is a bonanza for town planners, transport and property developers? We can apply simple tests. Will there be more social housing? What will happen to the poor and the homeless? Who will own the power, and communications and transportation networks? Where will my nearest hospital be? These progressive, even visionary, programmes cannot ignore social exclusion, poverty and homelessness. We do not want a version with the rich living in gated or skyscraper communities with protection of various kinds. There are examples of this elitism operating even in the same building, with one entrance for the owners (leaseholders) and one for the ordinary rent payer.

It was not until 1959 that the infamous seven-foot wall in Oxford, nicknamed the "snob wall" was pulled down. In December 1934, the Urban Housing Company retaliated by building two walls to protect the owners of their homes from their "social inferiors" on the other side. The seven-foot-high brick walls, which had bundles of iron spikes on the top to discourage people from jumping over, divided Wentworth Road from Aldrich Road, and Carlton Road from Wolsey Road. They caused at least one riot. To some, it was simply another layer of insult on top of the elitism represented by Oxford University itself.[133]

The same phenomenon that we are describing is threatened in India:

> *Even with high prices, the conventional laws in India will not enable us to exclude millions of poor Indians from enjoying the privileges of such great infrastructure. Hence the police will need to physically exclude people from such cities, and they will need a different set of laws from those operating in the rest of India for them to be able to do so. Creating special enclaves is the only method of doing so.*[134]

There is no hope for new projects if they seem to be just another third-way pact between the corporate sector and national or local government. Smart cities are going to be, or should be, a test bed for participatory democracy. There was not much participatory democracy in the building of the Shard in London.

Despite moves towards and pressure for further devolution and localism, there is a growing sense that, in Europe, the government is more remote from local communities than ever. This is captured well by the term "democratic deficit", the title of this chapter. The term is used mostly to refer to the whole apparatus of the EU, the weakness of the European Parliament, the lack of real representation at the centre, and the hugely unwieldy committee structure. Here is the same irony that was hinted at in the introduction. Many inside the organisations probably think of themselves as a progressive elite, nudging member states towards carefully thought-out policies for the protection of the environment, workers' rights, food safety and so on. Special research calls are put out, which were drafted by the best brains in Europe, through which academia can link with industry to develop cutting-edge technologies. But something is wrong with the system when there is youth unemployment in Southern Europe, when the EU cannot decide how to cope with illegal immigrants, and when it was late with its response to COVID-19. I am absolutely not pro-Brexit, but I am certainly pro ending the democratic deficit.

The EU is also subjected to intensive lobbying on behalf of corporate interests. EU Integrity Watch's recent report claims this:

EU analysis of the 4,318 lobby meetings declared by the top tier of European Commission officials between December 2014 and June 2015 shows that more than 75 were with corporate lobbyists. This compares to 18 with NGOs [non-governmental organisations], 4 with think tanks and 2 with local authorities. Google, General Electric and Airbus are some of the most active lobbyists at this level, with 25 to 29 meetings each. Google and General Electric are also some of the biggest spenders in Brussels, each declaring EU lobby budgets of around 3.5 million per year.[135]

There has been much work on the spectrum of ways in which the citizen can engage with government, and we can now summarise this, drawing particularly on Arnstein's "ladder of citizen participation".[136] At one end, we have little or no participation or information about what is going on: "I read about it in the newspapers." Even when the intentions are the best, the establishment has a tendency towards secrecy, closing ranks and closing doors, as explained in a previous chapter. The next rung in our ladder could be called "information but nothing else". Within this, there is reasonably good information, official documents, academic papers, useful websites on specialised subjects, personal experiences on blogs and social media, and so on. In moving towards active participation, we find that here and there is what is called a "statutory right" to be consulted. Thus, if your neighbour applies to the local planning authority to build an extension to their house, you will have the right to be consulted. You will be informed and will have a set time in which to submit written objections or support. These rights exist whether the local authority or a non-profit housing association is involved, and where a private company is the landlord. This higher level of public involvement will include examples where there are less-well-defined and less-formal consultation standards; for example, standards covering unbiased analysis and the publication of the results of the consultation. Citizens can attend planning meetings and may be allowed to make a statement. They may also have private conversations with a planning officer, but the conversation and access may be restricted in such situations.

An interesting area is the relationship between the citizen and utility companies, including internet providers. In the UK, this relationship is less than perfect. A key point is the nature of contracts. Most people may not easily be able to put their hand on their contract with, say, an electricity supplier. Can any of us, for example, explain the precise obligation of the electricity supplier in the case of a blackout due to a storm? What is the repair time or compensation, if any, let alone any mention of duty of care?

If a company takes electricity, or indeed any service, from a supplier, there is a tightly contracted service level agreement

(SLA), with obligations on both sides laid out clearly. Of course, with a bit of effort, searching in the bottom drawer or on the web, a kind of SLA for a domestic customer can be found. In the UK, they are typically called "terms and conditions". The paragraphs describing the obligations on the customer to the utility greatly outnumber the obligations of the supplier to the customer. Get-out clauses make interesting reading. Here is a sentence adapted from the terms and conditions from one of our own domestic suppliers: we aim to provide a continuous, high-quality service but we do not guarantee either the quality of the service or that the service will be available at all times.

These matters may seem like just the cut and thrust of everyday life, but they contain valuable principles. Much of the citizen's dealing with the outside world is contract based, but there are many areas where this contract is extremely vague despite the existence of much background consumer-rights legislation. Try to tease out whether the terms and conditions offered by your utilities conform to the regulations.[137]

Rawls's strong emphasis on the nature of institutions must be right. Whether at community, city, regional, national or international level, their relationship to the public is critical and is not always coherent. Nevertheless, as distressing from the public point of view is the failure of the regulators to do the job that they were appointed to do. What angers the UK public about the financial crisis is not just the behaviour of the banks but also the light-touch regulation, the inertia of the Financial Standards Authority (now the Financial Conduct Authority [FCA]) that allowed it to happen, and the failure to prosecute those responsible.

Interestingly, the relationship between corporations and the citizen is not all bad. In fact, it began to improve in what may be called the "quality revolution" in the 1970s and 1980s, when many quite-pleasing slogans were coined: "the customer comes first", "delight the customer", "customer relationship management" and "stakeholder management". There are even societies and associations promoting these ideas. The movement had a radical effect on improving the safety and reliability of Western products in response to Japanese competition. It seems that the same very healthy attitudes are only just beginning to permeate through to the boardrooms of utilities and banks, and there is some suspicion that attitudes have regressed, with incidents such as passengers being dragged off airplanes.

A nice experiment is to put the name of a utility or bank into your favourite search engine, together with the phrase "customer charter". Such charters are a kind of shop window behind which the contract or terms and conditions are lodged. They cover issues such as complaint procedures. Although there seems to be a bewildering range of choices for services, the actual range may not be so wide and, more importantly, there is little scope for involvement or negotiation. In the UK, there is waiting on the telephone, which seems to be a national pastime, and endlessly filling in forms online. There are no real contract negotiations between domestic customer and supplier. The statutory right to be consulted, as mentioned previously, is written into law by definition and is part of elective democracy. We elect our Members of Parliament, and they make law, with a bit of help from the unelected House of Lords. We elect local councillors, to whom we make planning applications. But there is something beyond that called "participatory democracy", which takes many forms.

"Localism" in the UK, as a counterweight to globalisation, seems at first glance to encourage democracy and involvement at a local-community level. However, it can mean a way of bypassing the established electoral local government to favour privatisation. There are now public sector schools in the UK that are directly responsible to central government, and thus out of the hands of the local authority. This is a two-tier model, with some coming together at a very local level combined with a central inspectorate, which – in extremis – can take over management on the local level.

The situation is complicated where you have an agency such as the Environment Agency, which has powers that can affect, say, a rural area. The UK is increasingly afflicted with heavy storms, which cause flooded towns and villages in certain areas, leading to billions of pounds worth of damage. Local residents, local authorities, regional government, national government, the Environment Agency and the insurance companies continue to be involved. In many cases, flood protection has proved insufficient, and there have been complaints that investment had been inadequate or delayed. A particular complaint is connected with upstream run-off. Farmers upstream from the flooded towns have been favoured in flood-defence expenditure, some of which comes from the EU: a hard cow-versus-car choice. The point here is this is another example of localism: direct funding from the centre, which favours one sector of the community at the expense of another.

One issue with direct government-to-local or agency-to-local management is that the special features of the locality may not be taken into account adequately in the data capture for the modelling to make forecasts and in the day-to-day management, particularly in emergency situations. Extreme rainfall, probably due to climate change, may be only one reason for the floods. Upstream deforestation may be another. In the long term, it may be that areas of the country become uninhabitable because of flooding. The UK government was very late to take a local approach to the management of the COVID-19 pandemic.

Insurance companies are beginning to refuse to insure certain parties or to set exemption rates at affordable levels. In the US, so-called "force based" insurance policies have led to controversy. These policies arise when an existing insurance policy comes to an end, and the lender, the bank or the mortgage company, on realising that a property is in an increasingly high-risk area, arranges insurance through an insurance company to protect its loan on the property, but then passes the cost – which may be far higher than necessary – on to the customer.

Any such sacrifices should not be made without first having a coming together of all concerned, to try to avoid them. Hillside forestation, ponds, ditches, soil and wooden debris barriers can be used to slow the run-off from the hills. The cost of these is insignificant compared to the cost of property damage in the town downstream. It is also obvious that expenditure should be spent on implementing better modelling and prevention measures. A failure to do so would make any local population feel that there is a different policy operating at national level.

One paradox is that, in times of austerity, the central government may benefit from the altruism of citizens who feel it is their civic duty to fill any gaps revealed by scarcities. What needs to be avoided is the refusal to acknowledge that there are implicit policies at the national level, such as the failure to tax corporations adequately, that are based on the premise that charities will pick up the bill. This would be a return to the politics of Herbert Spencer: the survival of the fittest and charity for the rest. My objection here is not so much political as simply a fear that we will fail to deal properly with the hard choices. People will fall through the net. Patients will die, and flooded villages will end up derelict.

One of the issues for democracy in the UK is the outsourcing of decisions to regulatory agencies such as NICE, the Environment Agency and the FCA. These agencies are often bureaucratically remote from local communities. Furthermore, there is a more serious problem: that of the inappropriate and even corrupt influence of major vested interests in these agencies. This is "regulatory capture". The corruption can be direct, such as financial bribes, including offering plum jobs to civil servants on retirement, or indirect, such as in distorting the ethos of the agency towards that of the organisations being regulated. Sometimes, it is built in, such as the fact that the FCA is actually funded by the financial institutions being regulated.

Regulatory capture has a long history. It has been argued it is inevitable that, for example, powerful corporations will move more or less automatically to capture the appropriate regulator. We find a subculture of economics that has been built on this inevitability, including mathematical theories. Ironically, regulatory capture has progressed in parallel with the area of corporate social responsibility (CSR). At the same time as the banks are clearly having undue influence on the FCA and Her Majesty's Revenue and Customs (HMRC), they are happily engaged in charitable activities.

Maybe one should set up a hypothesis of one's own. Here it is. There are roughly two kinds of corporations: the good and the bad. The good have high CSR and indulge in low regulatory capture (RC). The bad have low CSR combined with high RC. After reviewing the literature carefully, one designs one's own indices for both CSR and RC. The two are then plotted, with the statistician's beloved "unit of measurement" being a corporation or company, and it is hoped that there is a negative correlation, so that one's good–bad hypothesis is accepted and one's paper published. One might then combine the two indices to define a new "goodness metric". On the other hand, suppose that in the overconfident rush to publish and to enhance one's curriculum vitae (CV), and with only a few days to go before the submission deadline for the journal's special issue for one's new and definitive paper, one finds no correlation. Then one panics and works hard to say that one's hypothesis of rough separation between good and bad was rejected and that most corporations are engaged in both, and one's paper is rejected.

An agency or regulatory body is created by statute, enshrining in law its duties and its relationship to the private and public sectors. These may be partly related to the public good, such as in areas of safety and environmental protection, but may also relate to support for an industry. Regulatory capture can impede the agency's performance of its duties in subtle ways. It can deliberately introduce delays, rely too much on agreements for industry to self-manage, and plead lack of resources to conduct inspections or surveys.

This essay is concerned with the public good and, particularly, with individuals being sacrificed for the public good, often without decent compensation, if any. But when an agency has been captured, it may not work for the public good, but instead favour particular interests. It is likely that individuals will suffer more in these cases. Such cases lead to calls to abolish an agency, split it into several parts, change its name and so on. However, that is no solution, or rather it is a solution that may favour the very organisations being regulated.

The point is to *stop the regulatory capture*. The organisations that are there to protect the public may need to be protected themselves. And, to repeat, they all need to have a duty of care enshrined into their constitutions and, as in the Armed Services Covenant, should have to report every year on how that duty has been performed. In this way, these regulators could help to define the social contract. How wonderful it would be if the

FCA were the first regulator after that for the armed services to enshrine all this into its constitution.

A government not willing to protect individuals from the side effects of actions that it claims are in the public good may also be one that does not defend the agencies whose duty is to defend the public. In that case, both the agency and the government itself may have been captured. Taxation is a good example. The government needs taxation to pay for the public good, but it then cuts back resources for the internal revenue service (HMRC in the UK), which then claims it does not have the resources to pursue large-scale corporate tax evasion. This is a vicious circle in which the only beneficiary is the corporation itself.

Although banned occasionally by the regulators from discriminating between their customers, insurance companies work hard to obtain information about their customers behaviour and lifestyle. There is recent evidence that insurance companies are tracking customers on social media in order to discover lifestyle details that may help them protect themselves from the risk of insuring individual customers. For years, point-of-sale data collected under customer loyalty cards by supermarkets has been used to arrange products around the store, and in the case of web-based sales, it has been used to suggest products to the customer and even to indicate if they have forgotten something from their regular list. These strategies might be considered to be a rather innocuous way to improve the market for products and to propel marketing into the big data era. However, it could be seen as an invasion of privacy undertaken by a Goliath corporation to skim more money out of customers.

In the insurance case, some customers may be offered cheaper deals, but many others will lose out because of some aspects of their behaviour, which may have nothing to do with what is being insured. Certainly, the customers themselves will have no knowledge of the mathematical model that uses their demographics and behaviour as input and outputs their risk. Other than ticking some box that allows the data to be used by goodness knows whom, all this is beyond any kind of SLA, terms and conditions, etc., which should be part of the relationship between the customer and supplier. The situation represents an unbalanced exchange.

How do socioeconomic theories on private–public partnership, the third-way globalisation and its accompanying risks, deal with situations in which huge streams of data extracted from web marketing and social media are used to promote private and one-sided contracts with customers? Ironically, it is not so much that Facebook itself should be highly regulated. The fact that Facebook is free neatly avoids any contract other than agreeing to some rudimentary terms and conditions of use. Rather, it is the fact that it provides a platform for the unregulated use of data that affects real contracts. It seems that this is closer to statistical arbitrage in the financial sector. Scurrying around looking for arbitrage opportunities seems equivalent to seeking personal-behaviour patterns, such as drinking 250ml glasses of New Zealand Chardonnay as opposed to a more moderate 170ml, all of which could be accorded a parameter in the subgroup of parameters in a customised causal-network model of social behaviour.

We need help. The project-based educational methods of Dewey put the imagination at the forefront of reasoning, as we have tried to explain in the introduction and Chapter 7. Dewey seeks an experimental method of enquiry, but one that immerses itself equally in "the large and constant features of human sufferings, enjoyments, trial, failures… genuine features of the world within which man lives",[138] and one that is not biased by some superimposed and inappropriate mathematical logic. He rejects the brutality of logical empiricism in favour of a more psychological and community-based approach, which we might today call "empathy".

I have not yet allowed myself a grand design, and I am somewhat envious of those such as Paul Mason who have allowed themselves to do so.[139] But let me have a go anyway. My wish is that we will be able to call this the second age of Dewey, "Dewey Two" or some such (I note with pleasure the presence of the John Dewey Society). I can do this without too much deep philosophical discussion, simply by giving his methods a modern slant. Dewey's aim, as I have just said, is to have a method that is scientific in a broad sense, but not anchored to any dogmatic propositions, and certainly not those of free-market economics or raw utilitarianism.

What would Dewey Two look like? I claim that it is already with us. For example, I discussed earlier what modern methods of causation look like in the medical and social sciences. They exist, but are hugely complicated. One has to guard against hidden confounders and biases, feedback in the causal pathways, and huge heterogeneity, because we are studying people in social and physical environments, all of which can change dynamically and sometimes dramatically. Any successful method also has to understand and make use of the difference between passive observation and active experimentation, and between causation and correlation. All these were major concerns of Dewey. Here is an unlikely example taken from a recommendation from the US Food and Drug Administration when struggling with these ideas.

An adaptive design for a medical device clinical study is defined as a clinical study design that allows for prospectively planned modifications based on accumulating study data without undermining the study's integrity and validity. In nearly all situations, in order to preserve the integrity and validity of a study, modifications should be prospectively planned and described in the clinical study protocol prior to initiation of the study. However, in some specific circumstances, modifications to the design after the study begins can be scientifically valid if they are made without knowledge of the outcome results by treatment.[140]

Note the inherent dynamics and the notion of adaptivity, both of which are at the centre of Dewey's philosophy. The modern world is full of activities that speak to social complexities: opinion polling, analysing point-of-sale data, social networks, insurance companies wanting to learn who we really are, and the way that we hope to learn new "features" and so-called "emergent phenomena" from big data. But to complete a design of Dewey Two, we have to include what we have learned about new types of participatory and deliberative democracy. We are all part of the experiment. One can hope that this is the antidote to the continuing elitism and secrecy of governments, and that it will help us understand the narratives of the sacrificed and oppose the way in which decisions taken in the "safe spaces" of government then emerge as choices forced on the citizenry by local commandants.

At the level of government, we see various major themes operating, which are part ideological, part financial and a mixture of the two. One good example we have seen already is the constitution of the NHS. Its first articles retain some of the idealism of its foundation, but then we have a new reference to the taxpayer in the new Article 6. There the taxpayer takes on the role of an allegorical figure, like "Hope" and "Charity" symbolising thrift and austerity. He or she is a moral figure who is only accorded a one-dimensional personality, mumbling continuously (as if in a Monty Python film), "Less tax, less tax."

But the actual taxpayer is a real citizen and is not one-dimensional – a fact that I have gone to some length to emphasise, courtesy of Ruskin and Dickens. This person has altruism, empathy, imagination and fancy. UK citizens donate over £10 billion to charities every year, and for this, the World Giving Index places the UK seventh in the world. Also, the figures do not include the huge contribution of unpaid voluntary work for charities. The UK's citizens are especially generous when giving to appeals such as Live Aid, Comic Relief and Children in Need. We are not ostentatious about it, and discussing it is embarrassing; it is a kind of reflex altruism that stems, in my opinion, from some deep sense of duty – civic duty. In the UK, this strange and eccentric country, asking someone what they give to charity is like asking them how old they are or about their love life. Everything in Albion is an embarrassment.

This altruism is in stark contrast to the self-interested stereotype promoted by the government, but it is our altruism that the government has a special interest in: it pays charities to provide services at the local level. This has led to a wide discussion of the role of charities. There are complaints that the large charities have become too corporate, resembling – and having too close a relationship with – private sector firms involved in the same work. This includes comments about the large salaries of the charities' senior executives. There is evidence that there is a moral price to pay, with charities being threatened with the withdrawal of government contracts if they continue to campaign or are critical of their paymasters. The UK government had to abandon a plan for a gagging bill to stop any funds that have been given to a charity by the government that they infer is being used to campaign or put pressure on governments. There is a sense in which charities have been partially "captured", in the sense of regulatory capture.

The kind of taxpayer-v-citizen double standard that operates in the government's approach to charities is part of a wider phenomenon. As I have said, scarcity and austerity at the top level are pushed down to the local level and to the individual citizen, which leads to forced choices. This push-down is accompanied by a cloak of secrecy, which Rawls refers to as "invisible rationing", out of sight and out of mind. Decisions are, by default, taken by experts such as doctors and charity workers. We talk about the outsourcing of risk, or risk allocation; for example, in large capital projects.

At its most profound, we have a kind of fracturing and outsourcing of ethics itself, and this seems more or less to be the status quo. It is "positive" in the sense of "positive economics"; such economics would, for example, take scarcity as a given. But even if every expert had a degree in ethics with a minor in economics, it would not be enough. The normative theory should open up all the burdens of judgement to wider public deliberation. Being a doctor is not the same as being a patient, however strong the empathy. Making decisions about who may use a food bank is not the same as using a food bank. We are not asking for some kind of Maoist cultural revolution, just a broadening of the deliberation.

Deliberative democracy is a concept that is based partly in traditional approaches to democracy and also in a dissatisfaction with existing forms – not so much in what they are, but in their scope. One such dissatisfaction is with the lack of openness that I have referred to before. The free and frank discussions should not be the privilege of government decision-makers. Simply, from a decision-making point of view, diversity of opinion and experience tends to lead to better decisions. This has been shown by serious research, and its opposite is well captured by the concept of group think and the wider study of cognitive biases, such as overoptimism. Looking at the dreadful blunders made by various UK governments, a typical pattern can be seen of bad decisions made by a small coterie of ministers and advisors, with huge overoptimism and divorced from the realities. Sadly, we can now add the handling of COVID-19 to the list.

Here, the realities that concern us most are those everyday realities of human life. Our thesis is that decisions made at a high level ignore or deliberately avoid the multitude of hard choices that they force on a day-to-day basis. Some of these are the result of poverty, such as having to choose between heating and eating. But even if poverty is affected by austerity decisions, heating is affected by the cost of fuel, which is in the domain of a regulator, and eating is affected by supermarkets, which have another regulator. Both regulators tell us that one of their jobs is to help make the market more competitive. Good on them, but until they achieve this idealistic aim, they need to control the price hikes that come from these quasi-monopolies.

What is missing from this picture is *community*. Let us track, as Dewey might, a parent throughout the working day. They may have a job, say, in the private sector; they wake up in the morning, take the children to school, may travel to work, shop, talk to friends on their mobile phone, visit an elderly relation, send some emails, or read a website or two. A busy day. During that day, they are householders, they are members of a local community, they may be members of a parent-teacher association, they are commuters, they are users of social media and the web, and they are carers. On the same day, they are operating as a member of several different communities; that is, groups of other people with common interests. If they cycle to work, they probably feel an affinity with the other hard-done-by cyclists, say, in London. They may stop at their favourite cycle shop and chat to other cyclists they hardly know, all of whom may encourage each other to join a campaign about cycle lanes, and at home, they may access the cycle campaign website. They may just be able to catch the late news to hear that the government has plans for the care allowance for the elderly and are therefore concerned because of their own elderly relative. Dewey has said all this:

> *The world of action is a world of which the individual is one limit, and humanity the other; between them lie all sorts of associative arrangements of lesser and larger scope, families, friendships, schools, clubs, organisations for making or distributing goods, for gathering and supplying commodities; activities politically organised by parishes, wards, villages, cities, countries, states, nations. Every maladjustment in relations among these institutions and associated activities means loss and friction in the relations between individuals; and thereby introduces defect, division, and restriction into the various powers which constitute an individual. All harmonious cooperation among them means a fuller life and greater freedom of thought and action for the individual person.*[141]

We need Dewey on two fronts: democracy and methodology. Some authors credit him with having many of the ideas now captured in deliberative democracy. He was probably the most prolific writer on democracy in the twentieth century. It was much harder for his ideas on methodology to get accepted, because of attacks on his work by Bertrand Russell and others in what became what is now sometimes called the "Russell-Dewey debate".[142] Dewey had the disadvantage of not being a professional logician but on the other hand he had the strong tradition of the American Pragmatists, led by William James and Charles Saunders Peirce (Peirce almost discovered information theory, contributed to Bayesian methods and invented optimum experimentation, which he called the "economy of experiment" and has become something of a modern cult). Dewey's ideas may be much closer to what is needed today than either of the two tracks of twentieth-century philosophy – the "logical atomism" of Russell and others, and the pure "falsification" of Karl Popper – both giving, in my opinion, a too-clinical and rationalist view of truth.

I have touched on some of the difficulties already. In Chapter 3, I mentioned the problem of real distributions, such as income distributions and theoretical distributions, which are some kind of idealisation of reality. The other problem was that of combining expert judgement with data; perhaps this should be called combining expert *belief* with data. The Bayesian methods may be the best game in town and have a nice axiomatic foundation. Put naïvely, this can be summarised as (prior belief) × (data) = (posterior belief). The correct version is a rather beautiful formula, Bayes rule. But to be highfalutin, this does not really deal with our existential relationship with reality. After all, our beliefs are buried somewhere in our brains, and the outside world, which as realists we believe in, is, well, something else. What Dewey says is that our whole relationship with reality is part of the issue and it cannot just be summarised in a few axioms. Reality is very complex. Today, we might say that the more big data we gather, the more complexity and uncertainty seems to grow, not diminish. Dewey declares that doing science is a problem-solving activity, truth lies in our ability to solve conundrums via a mixture of belief and experiment he calls "inquiry" and solving the problem leads to a type of understanding that is operationally useful – hence the term "pragmatism".

Nevertheless, Dewey's most important idea for us here is that of community. Dewey considers science to be a community activity – a community of problem solvers. Fortunately, inspirationally, he takes the same ideas over to democracy. Democracy at its best should be a community exercise, with communities working to solve problems in an open, deliberative and experimental manner. There is a very strong analogy between the domination of public policy by simplistic utilitarian formulae and the domination of science by what we were taught by Thomas Kuhn to call "paradigms". We see policy and science coming together right now with the COVID-19 crisis. As I write we see the failure to model adequately the local behaviour of the virus comes with over-centralised decision-making and a rather pompous attitude to local communities.

One consequence of the failure to try continually to understand our relationship to reality is a failure of *attention* – the failure to look in the right place to help us understand the problems. We see a stark reminder of this every day on the news. We see the data on the epidemic and broad instructions from the government, and then we hear the personal narratives of the patients and their families. We see the risks but we also see the victims. If we are lucky we hear from the communities, be it a care home provider or local councillor complaining about a lack of information or equipment. What we get from government is one-way, top-to-bottom directives and the brutal pseudo-rationality of a primitive cost-benefit analysis, with a sour dressing of blame. We must not take this attitude into dealing with climate change.

Dewey's view is that society is a multi-faceted web of communities and it should be dynamic and evolving, through continually discussing and re-examining in an organic way. He was very critical of fixed methodologies in science, and favoured a similar experimental approach. This was also his approach to education, where he was particularly famous for saying that education should include preparation for citizenship of the kind that would prosper within his organic version of democracy. He was against the elitism of the Ivy League, Oxbridge and the Grands Ecoles in which educated elites are prepared to keep the governing class topped up. He was criticised for being idealist and for not being more specific about how we get from the present to the all-inclusive, participatory democracy he envisioned. Nonetheless, his answer – as it should be for us – is that customs and procedures would evolve as part of the very process of community involvement. Learning about and being an actor in society means, first, operating within a community; second, reaching an experimental, dynamic and cross-hatched version of understanding; and, above all, adopting a democratic approach of mutual respect. It should include imagination, fancy and empathy.

Even without formal structures for participatory or deliberative democracy, we see how the internet is already meeting some of the demand for social interaction via social media and new mass forms of cause-led pressure groups, such as "38 Degrees" in the UK. Some politicians and civil servants may want to occupy a safe space away from the scrutiny of the citizen, but receiving a petition with 150,000 signatures just before they go into their free and frank deliberation behind closed doors must be quite chastening.

A good society – a safe-but-free society – should endeavour to remove painful or even terrible choices, not hide behind a macho position that life is hard and hard choices have to be made. Of course life is hard and hard choices have to be made, but our position is that a test, and quite possibly the supreme test, of a good society is whether or not it tries to eliminate the need to make the choices.

The most difficult hurdle of all standing in our way is the perceived necessity for winners and losers. There is a fundamental difference between the kind of healthy competition in sport and business (which can exploit common interest and team spirit), and the fundamental structural inequalities imposed by accidents of birth or geography. Going along with the idea of winners and losers is like tossing a coin to determine who lives and who dies, and saying that is fair because everybody has the same chance before the toss of the coin. We don't have to play this game. Whenever hard choices are thrust upon us by politicians or their servants, pleading scarcity or appealing to the public good, we should be suspicious or at least curious.

If this essay has no benefit other than to draw attention to where the sacrifices are made in modern society, then at least we should know where to look by now. We look everywhere where there are cash limits and scarcity is discussed, and we see who is talking about them. We look to see where proportionality is used to infringe basic rights, and where politicians are using phrases such as "hard decisions" without saying who is affected and by how much. Today, we have the web, which reveals all eventually, once we have the relevant search list. For every one of the situations discussed in this essay, and many more, we can track down those victims or potential victims. We can make our own map of the wild frontier. In fact, maps showing regional inequalities already exist; e.g. for poverty, heat demand, life expectancy and pollution. For the world, the maps will show the scarcity; e.g. where there are water shortages for want of pipes and political will.

It is clear that, however worthy and progressive the elected government tries to be, and however well-informed and independent the civil service and its agencies are, more public involvement is essential. We need new forms of public participation, particularly in places where the sacrifices and choices are to be made. It will not be surprising, and is to be welcomed in fact, if victims spearhead the pressure groups, because we need to hear their stories above all: the narratives of sacrifice.

If we really cannot eliminate the hard choices, then we should mitigate them at least. The sacrificed should be compensated, and the compensation should be generous and swift. There should not be complex, slow and expensive bureaucratic hurdles. If we have found out who the sacrificed are, there should not be years of waiting to establish the obvious. Without a generosity of spirit towards the sacrificed in one area, they will suffer more, which will undermine the good work done to eliminate hard choices in other areas. Absolutely fundamental is removing the complacency, the idea that the status quo is okay, and that it is okay to sacrifice a few for the greater good.

Of course, resources are limited, even though we know that talk of scarcity may be influenced by vested interests. Choices have to be made, but the choices presented may not be what they seem. They may be presented at the margin, almost deliberately, to avoid looking at the wider ethical environment in which all choices are embedded. In this wider environment, huge political forces operate. One such is against taxation. A possibly lasting victory of the free-market economists, to whom this volume has dished out a certain amount of abuse, is the fear of politicians of all persuasions of increasing taxation of the better off. To make a final use of our topographical metaphor, those in the counting houses of utilitarian ethics and the exchange houses of free-market economics need to get out from behind their desks and join the rescue parties to save people from the wild frontiers, where their theories can lead to brutal, and even illegal, decisions about life and death.

There are many books about the future of democracy, each with a different emphasis and some trying to come up with the answer to questions such as what happens as globalisation declines, how to cope with the new age when robots will take our jobs, how to handle fake news on the internet and how to deal with a populist swing to the right. These are all good questions, but they are not answered here. Some writers go back to Karl Marx's analysis of capitalism, some are based on the deliberations of well-endowed think tanks, and some (the ones I prefer) talk about enhancing local democracy and worker participation.

We have to see what is wrong before we can fix it, and we perhaps must look for solutions that exist or at least that we have access to. In Chapter 1, I talked about all the agencies and ALBs already charged with improving aspects of public life, by whom ethical decisions are made every day. We can track the ABCD committee structure we described in the introduction. If we are not sure about something, we can look it up on our search engine. We can, with some degree of confidence, check facts on Wikipedia, Google Scholar and the arXiv, and can buy important books quickly online. We have access to reports from the select committees of the House of Commons and answers to parliamentary questions.

If there is a single answer to why all this is not all working, and why people are being sacrificed it must be this: *those charged with monitoring and improving public life are not doing their job.* We can ask what the reasons for this are: Are they underfunded? Do they have the right terms of reference? Are they given no teeth? Are they ignorant and unworldly? Do they lack empathy for ordinary people? Are they lazy and prefer to procrastinate? Is there no legal accountability?

But we know the real answer, even if we cannot say here and now, as other texts do, what the future should be or how to get there. The answer is that the people in this web of organisations are frightened. It is fear that stops people doing things. And we even know something about what they are frightened of: they fear the voice of the victims. It is so much easier to hide behind an old theory, equipped with probability and risk theories, and with nice, strong equals signs. It is so much easier not to respond to an invitation to appear on television to explain what is going on, and so much easier to outsource the scary ethical decisions to others.

If ever the COVID-19 crisis settles down to a manageable level, we will still have the climate change issue, terrible inequalities, weak economies and wars. The balance between central, local and community-based politics is shifting. For COVID-19, the patience of governments with citizens (in terms of distancing and self-care) and, conversely, that of citizens with the governments (as they wallow in secrecy, poor management and poor communication) is weakening. Both are wondering what the future is. The clichés mount up: a new paradigm, rethinking the future, managing the risk, understanding the uncertainty, and the end of globalisation. But perhaps all of these are valiant attempts to cope with the future. If we can add "no sacrifice" to the list, then this author would be happy.

The good news is that much may be fixable. Of course, not if you are a small-state guru and you like to cash starve the NHS and the regulators, not if you let those being regulated take over the regulators, and not if you issue health and safety targets that you then ignore wilfully. But if your terms of reference are to plant trees and protect wetlands, then plant and protect. If your terms of reference are to mend leaks in water mains, then do the mending. If your job is to protect care homes from a virus , then do it. Do it and don't blame it on the victims of your inaction or mistakes. Do the job you are paid for, without fear and favour. If your job forces you to make horrible choices, then don't hide in your office, laboratory or home, go to the rooftop and blow the whistle!

Index

Endnotes

1   The poem 'I see the Four-fold Man' is part of William Blake's *Jerusalem The Emanation of the Giant Albion*, which is best known from the hymn also called 'Jerusalem'.

2   "… to the greatest benefit of the least advantaged, consistent with the just savings principle." Rawls (2009).

3   Nozick (1974).

4   See the National Audit Office report: https://www.nao.org.uk/wp-content/uploads/2016/05/ Departments-oversight-of-arms-length-bodies-a-comparative-study.pdf

5   Palin conveyed her views in a Facebook entry on 7 August 2009. From then on, the debate has held the tag "the death panel myth".

6   Sophie's Choice is centred on a scene in Auschwitz where Sophie has just arrived with her ten-year-old son and her seven-year-old daughter. A sadistic doctor, presumably modelled on Doctor Mengele, tells her that she can only bring one of her children; one will be allowed to live while the other is to be killed. Styron (2004).

7   https://downloads.bbc.co.uk/radio4/reith2020/ Reith_2020_Lecture_3_transcript.pdf

8   The history of NICE makes interesting reading; see Timmins et al. (2017).

9   There are many useful and critical guides to QALYs. A good example is Prieto and Sacristán (2003).

10 https://www.nice.org.uk/about/who-we-are/our-principles. This document contains a useful list of other documents such as the NICE charter and NICE constitution.

11 This is response to an academic report by the NICE director Sir Andrew Dillon: https://www.nice.org.uk/news/blog/ carrying-nice-over-the-threshold

12 See the following for a review of WTP methods: Breidert et al. (2006). Road safety is another area where WTP has a foothold alongside other methods such as, value of a statistical life (VSL) and value of risk reduction (VRR) (discussed in Chapter 3).

13 A simple view of social welfare theory is that it is a rather mathematical development of the tension between individual choice and group choice. Famous examples are Arrow's impossibility theorem and the critical work of Sen (1991).

14 The National Health Service Commissioning Board and Clinical Commissioning Groups (Responsibilities and Standing Rules) Regulations 2012. UK Statutory Instruments 2012, No. 2996, PART 7.
    The document say "disinvestments should be considered along with investments".

15 Daniels et al. (2013).

16 Knight et al. (2020).

17 The document is available at: https://www.gov.uk/ government/publications/the-nhs-constitution-for england/the-nhs-constitution-for-england

18 Hansard, House of Commons, series 5, vol. 487 (23 April 1951). This speech was made two days after his resignation as Minister of Health, as which he founded the NHS.

19 The Taxpayers' Alliance was founded in 2004 by Matthew Elliot, a leading Eurosceptic. It has been accused of being a right-wing front organisation and is less than open about its sources of funding.

20 https://www.nice.org.uk/news/article/using-nice-s-approach-to-base-policy-decisions-on-evidence-could-help-save-billions

21 Blake, Coleridge and Wordsworth are romantic poets, and they are sometimes also called poets of the imagination and fancy. It is important for us that these ideas re-emerge as components of the concept of empathy and in the work of John Dewey. Failures of imagination have been held responsible for major disasters: McCaul (2016), Jensen III (2007).

22 European Convention on Human Rights (19 April 2017). https://www.equalityhumanrights.com/en/what-european-convention-human-rights

23 Nord (1995).

24 Llorente (1843).

25 Edwards v National Coal Board. (CA) Court of Appeal (1949) 1 All E. R. 743.

26 https://www.legislation.gov.uk/ukpga/1974/37/contents

27 Case C127-05 European Commission v United Kingdom.

28 The Stoiber Committee was called the "Action Programme for Reducing Administrative Burdens to Business in the EU". There were further initiatives such as the Regulatory Fitness and Performance Program (REFIT), as part of the EU's Growth Challenge. These were partly in response to pressure from David Cameron, the UK Prime Minister,

to cut red tape. The UK government commissioned an independent report, which recommended exempting the self-employed from health and safety regulations. See Lèfstedt (2011).

29 https://www.tuc.org.uk/news/workers-would-be-put-risk-stoiber-proposals-says-tuc

30 https://www.hse.gov.uk/economics/eauappraisal.htm. The figure of £1,296,000 is to be found in Table 1.

31 Nader(1965). Here is another famous quotation from Ralph Nader: "When do corporations begin to lose credibility? They fought Social Security, Medicare, auto safety. They fought every social justice movement in the country."

32 Nicolas Watt (5 January 2012). David Cameron takes aim at Britain's health and safety culture. *The Guardian*. https://www.theguardian.com/uk/2012/jan/05/cameron-targets-health-and-safety-rules

33 WTA and WTP can be seen as part of an economic theory that takes into account transaction cost and externalities. Needless to say, this has received its Nobel prizes; for example, to John Coase for the Coase theorem. The development has made a debatable contribution to public expenditure. For a review, see Butler and Garnett (2003).

34 For an excellent edited collection covering these issues see Chang (1997).

35 The "Rule of Rescue" or "Rescue Theory" has a foothold in the ethics related to resourcing. See the following: McKie and Richardson (2003).

36 Apte et al. (2015).

37 Piketty (2018).

38 As cited in Engle (2012).

39 Galbraith (1998).

40 https://www.un.org/en/universal-declaration-human-rights/

41 Thomson (1976).

42 Fink (2013). This dangerous territory of applying some kind of reverse triage in times of crisis has sprung up with COVID-19. See particularly the multi-author report, Emanuel et al. (2020).

43 Jones (2006).

44 World Economic Forum (WEF) (2019). The UK report is Exercise Cygnus, which the UK government has been accused of partly suppressing:https://www.england.nhs.uk/wp-content/uploads/2017/03/board-paper-300317-item-10.pdf

45 Again, reverse triage. The COVID-19 Decision Support Tool discriminates on grounds of both age and gender. You collect points in various categories. Here is an example: (i) male gender = 0 points (female = 1 point); (ii) age 71–75 = 4 points; (iii) clinical frailty of vulnerable = 4 points; and (iv) co-morbidity of hypertension = 1 point. This gives a total of 9, which is greater than the cut-off of 8, so no ICU for you. http://prod-upp-image-read.ft.com/765d3430-7a57-11ea-af44-daa3def9ae03

46 Awad et al. (2018).

47 Knight (1921) and see also Kay and King (2020).

48 Armstrong and Carroll (2017).

49 O'Hara (2016).

50 Association of British Insurers, (2014). *Concordat and moratorium on genetics and insurance.*

51 Broome (1978).

52 Health and Safety Executive (2015). ALARP at "a glance".

53 Ross (2019).

54 Feyerabend (1993).

55 Jack Ashley's speech was during the second reading of the Vaccine Damages Bill; see the following: Hansard, House of

Commons, vol. 962 (5 February 1979).

56 The code plus discussion appears in Shuster (1997).

57 Fox (2016).

58 See the "Rapid Response" by Wendy E. Stephen to the paper, Moberly (2017).

59 Holland, M. S. (2017). Liability for vaccine injury: The United States, the European Union, and the developing world. *Emory LJ*, *67*, 415.

60 Cohan (2007).

61 Martin (2004).

62 The Law Commission. *Administrative redress: public bodies and the citizen.* Consultation paper, No. 322. For a critical commentary see Percival, R. (2019).

63 The extract is taken from a "rough English translation" of the District Court decision in the case of The Urgenda Foundation v. The State of the Netherlands, 24 June 2015. Section 4.53. The judgement against the Dutch Government was broadly upheld and nuanced by the Appeal Court and the Supreme Court. There has been considerable subsequent writing, e.g. van Zeben (2015) and de Jong (2015).

64 Hills (2012).

65 A thoughtful article discussing the interplay between corporate social responsibility (CSR) and various forms of compliance is Sinkovics et al. (2016).

66 http://www.respect.international/french-corporate-duty-of-vigilance-law-english-translation/

67 Territory, Australian Capital, "Civil Law (Wrongs) Act 2002". New South Wales (NSW) Civil Liability Act (2002). https://www.youngslist.com.au/docs/the-government-s-duty-of-care--november-2015.pdf https://publications.parliament.uk/pa/ld201617/ldselect/ldfinexcl/132/13202.htm

Australian Capital: "We recommend that the Financial Services and Markets Act 2000 should be amended, in order to introduce a requirement for the FCA to make rules setting out a reasonable duty of care for financial services providers to exercise towards their customers".

68 https://www.fca.org.uk/publication/discussion/dp-18-05.pdf

69 A private member's Financial Duty of Care Bill [HL] 2019 "made no further progress".

70 Taylor, C. (2011). *Armed Forces Covenant* (Standard note SN/IA/5979). Government Publication.

71 ICISS (2001). Some follow up reports and papers are Evan et al. (2001), Welsh et al. (2002) and Arbour (2008).

72 Ruskin (1985).

73 MacIntyre (2013).

74 Gourevitch and Rousseau (2018).

75 ibid.

76 ibid.

77 ibid.

78 Gandhi (1983).

79 Dickens (1996). First edition (1854).

80 Nussbaum (1997). In the preface, Nussbaum writes "Our society is full of refusals to imagine one another with empathy and compassion, refusals from which none of us is free". Her Chapter 2 is titled "Fancy".

81 ibid.

82 Fesmire (2003).

83 Sen, A., 1997. *Resources, Values, and Development*. Harvard University Press.

84 Malthus et al. (1992).

85 The term "*Nachtwächterstaat*" was coined by the German Ferdinand Lassalle, who used it to criticise anti-state conservatives, but that did not stop it being used in a

positive sense.

86 de Jong and Quade (1967).

87 Thomas et al. (2006).

88 This is one of the more breathtaking ghost rides in the ethics fairground: Hardwig (1997).

89 Dickens (1997).

90 Lerner Simmons (1966). Observer's reaction to the "innocent victim": compassion or rejection? *Journal of Personality and Social Psychology, 4*(2), p.203.

91 Lambert et al. (1998).

92 Offer (2010).

93 Hofstadter (1992).

94 Sunstein (1987).

95 Nozick (1974).

96 Katz (2013).

97 Pillutla et al. (2018).

98 Dworkin (2002).

99 Horkheimer et al (2002).

100 Girard (1965).

101 Dodson and Schmalzbauer (2005).

102 Dumouchel (2017).

103 Department of Defence (2020).

104 Protocol I to the 1949 Geneva Conventions (AP I), Articles 57(2)(a)(iii) and 57(2)(b)

105 One can read how proportionality is built into the ethics of war in this useful and careful report: Gillard (2018).

106 GICHD (2018).

107 DARPA (2019).

108 This is the still available BBC sponsored WW2 People's War Project, Archive List: V-1s and V-2s. https://www.bbc.co.uk/history/ww2peopleswar/categories/c54649/

109 Chamayou (2015).

110 ibid.

111 Walzer (2015).

112 This quotation appears in McIntyre (2019).

113 https://dominiccummings.com/tag/drones/

114 Snow (2013).

115 This quotation is from the ruling by Judge Keith in case: Detroit Free Press v. Ashcroft, 303 F. 3d 681 – Court of Appeals, 6th Circuit 2002, April 2002.

116 Available at https://www.legislation.gov.uk/ukpga/2000/36/contents

117 King and Crewe (2014).

118 Cobain (2016).

119 https://www.gov.uk/government/publications/independent-commission-on-freedom-of-information-report

120 https://www.roadmap2050.eu/reports

121 Aston (2019).

122 Setzer and Byrnes (2019).

123 National Academies of Sciences, Engineering, and Medicine, 2016. *Attribution of Extreme Weather Events in the Context of Climate Change.* National Academies Press.

124 Shepherd et al (2018). Here is additional work on the topic:Lloyd and Oreskes (2018) and National Academies of Sciences, Engineering, and Medicine (2016).

125 UNEP (2015).

126 Judt (2011).

127 ibid.

128 Beck et al. (1992).

129 Giddens (1999).

130 Turner (2017).

131 Knox (2011).

132 The EU Smart Cities programme, with which this author has been involved, covers a significant range of projects. A

recent document is https://www.smarter-together.eu/eu-smart-cities-and-communities

133 Williams (2009).

134 Statement by Laveesh Bhandari of Indicus Analytics at the Smart Cities Summit in Mumbai, January 2015. See also Thomas (2019).

135 Transparency International with Integrity Watch monitors the billion-euro lobbying industry in the EU.

136 Arnstein (1969).

137 *Which?* magazine has useful advice on consumer protection.

138 Quoted in Hook (1977).

139 Mason (2016).

140 This is an extract from a developing series of guidance documents from the FDA and is titled: Adaptive Designs for Medical Device Clinical Studies: https://www.fda.gov/media/92671/download

141 Dewey and Tufts (1932).

142 Two accessible books on Dewey's philosophy of science are Tiles (1988) and Burke (1994).

References

Apte, J. S., Marshall, J. D., Cohen, A. J., & Brauer, M. (2015). Addressing global mortality from ambient PM2. 5. *Environmental science & technology*, *49*(13), 8057-8066.

Arbour, L. (2008). The responsibility to protect as a duty of care in international law and practice. *Review of International Studies*, 445-458.

Armstrong, A., & Carroll, M. (2017). Gambling activity in Australia. *Melbourne, Australia: Australian Gambling Research Centre, Australian Institute of Family Studies.*

Arnstein, S. R. (1969). A ladder of citizen participation. *Journal of the American Institute of Planners*, *35*(4), 216-224.

Aston, P. (2019). *On Inequality and Climate Change*. Interview, Chatham House.

Awad, E., Dsouza, S., Kim, R., Schulz, J., Henrich, J., Shariff, A., & Rahwan, I. (2018). The moral machine experiment. *Nature*, *563*(7729), 59-64.

Beck, U., Lash, S., & Wynne, B. (1992). *Risk Society: Towards a New Modernity* (Vol. 17). Sage.

Breidert, C., Hahsler, M., & Reutterer, T. (2006). A review

of methods for measuring willingness-to-pay. *Innovative Marketing, 2*(4), 8-32.

Broome, J. (1978). Trying to value a life. *Journal of Public Economics, 9*(1), 91-100.

Burke, T. (1994). *Dewey's New Logic: A Reply to Russell.* University of Chicago Press.

Butler, M. R., & Garnett, R. F. (2003). Teaching the Coase Theorem: are we getting it right?. *Atlantic Economic Journal, 31*(2), 133-145.

Chamayou, G. (2015). *Drone Theory.* Penguin UK.

Chang, R. (Ed.) (1997). *Incommensurability, Incomparability, and Practical Reason.* Harvard University Press.

Cobain, I. (2016). *The History Thieves: Secrets, Lies and the Shaping of a Modern Nation.* Portobello Books.

Cohan, J. A. (2007). Private and public necessity and the violation of property rights. *NDL Rev., 83,* 651.

Daniels, T., Williams, I., Robinson, S., & Spence, K. (2013). Tackling disinvestment in health care services. The views of resource allocators in the English NHS. *Journal of Health Organization and Management, 27*(6), 762–780.

DARPA (2019). Creating technological breakthroughs and new capabilities for national security.

Defence Advanced Research Project Agency.

de Jong, E. R. (2015). Dutch State Ordered to Cut Carbon Emissions. *Eur. J. Risk Reg., 6,* 448.

de Jong, F & Quade, W. (1967). Dimensional analysis for economists. Contributions to economic analysis; 50. North Holland.

Department of Defence (2020). Department of Defence Dictionary of Military and Associated Terms. Office of the Chairman of the Joint Chiefs of Staff, DOD Dictionary of Military and Associated Terms (Washington DC: The Joint

Staff, June 2020).

Dewey, J., & Tufts, J. H. (1932). *Ethics* (rev. ed.). New York: H. Holt and company.

Dickens, C. (1996). *Hard Times*. Broadview Press.

Dodson, L., & Schmalzbauer, L. (2005). Poor mothers and habits of hiding: Participatory methods in poverty research. *Journal of Marriage and Family*, *67*(4), 949-959.

Dumouchel, P. (2017). The Barren Sacrifice. In *The Palgrave Handbook of Mimetic Theory and Religion* (pp. 279-285). Palgrave Macmillan.

Dworkin, R. (2002). *Sovereign Virtue: The Theory and Practice of Equality*. Harvard University Press.

Emanuel, E. J., Persad, G., Upshur, R., Thome, B., Parker, M., Glickman, A., Zhang, C., Boyle, C., Smith, M. and Phillips, J. P., (2020). Fair allocation of scarce medical resources in the time of Covid-19. N.

Engl, J. Med, 2020; 382:2049-2055.

Engle, E. (2012). The history of the general principle of proportionality: An overview. *Dartmouth LJ*, *10*, 1.

European Union. *Energy Policy*, *52*, 563-572.

Evan, G., Sahnoun, M., Côté-Harper, G., Hamilton, L., & Ignatieff, M. (2001). *Responsibility to Protect: Report of the International Commission on Intervention and State Sovereignty*. IDRC, Ottawa, ON, CA.

Fesmire, S. (2003). *John Dewey and Moral Imagination: Pragmatism in Ethics*. Indiana University Press.

Feyerabend, P. (1993). *Against Method*. Verso.

Fink, S. (2013). *Five Days at Memorial: Life and Death in a Storm-ravaged Hospital*. Atlantic Books Ltd.

Fox, R. (2016). *Helen's Story: A Routine Vaccination Ruined My Daughter's Life Forever. This is The Inspiring Story of How I Took on The Government… And Won*. Kings Road Publishing.

Galbraith, J. K. (1998). *The Affluent Society*. Houghton Mifflin Harcourt.

Gandhi, M. K. (1983). Autobiography: The story of my experiments with the truth. Dover.

GICHD (2018). MK 82 Aircraft Bomb, Geneva International Centre for Humanitarian Demining.

Giddens, A. (1999). Risk and responsibility. *Mod. L. Rev.*, *62*, 1.

Gillard, E. C. (2018). *Proportionality in the Conduct of Hostilities: the Incidental Harm Side of Proportionality Assessments*. Technical Report, Chatham House Report, 2018.

Girard, R. (1965). Deceit, desire, and the novel. *The Novel: An Anthology of Criticism and Theory 1900–2000*, 294-314.

Gourevitch, V., & Rousseau, J. J. (2018). *Rousseau: The Social Contract and Other Later Political Writings*. Cambridge University Press.

Hale, D. J. (Ed.) (2009). *The Novel: An Anthology of Criticism and Theory 1900-2000*. John Wiley & Sons.

Hardwig, J. (1997). Is there a duty to die?. *Hastings Center Report*, *27*(2), 34-42.

Hills, J. (2012). Getting the measure of fuel poverty: Final Report of the Fuel Poverty Review.

Hofstadter, R. (1992). *Social Darwinism in American Thought* (Vol. 16). Beacon Press.

Holland, M. S. (2017). Liability for vaccine injury: The United States, the European Union, and the developing world. *Emory LJ*, *67*, 415.

Hook, S. (1977). Reflections on the Metaphysics of John Dewey: "Experience and Nature". *Revue Internationale de Philosophie*, 313-328.

Horkheimer, M., Adorno, T. W., & Noeri, G. (2002). *Dialectic of Enlightenment*. Stanford University Press.

ICISS (2001). *The Responsibility to Protect: Report of the*

International Commission on Intervention and State Sovereignty. International Development Research Centre (Canada).

Jensen III, C. J. (2007). An Analysis of Failure: Pearl Harbor, 9/11, Hurricanes Katrina and Rita.

Jones, E. (2006). LMF: the use of psychiatric stigma in the Royal Air Force during the Second World War. *The Journal of Military History, 70*(2), 439-458.

Jong, F. J. de. (1967). Dimensional analysis for economists. North-Holland, Amsterdam.

Judt, T. (2011). *Ill Fares the Land: a Treatise on our Present Discontents.* Penguin UK.

Jung, R. E., Flores, R. A., & Hunter, D. (2016). A new measure of imagination ability: Anatomical brain imaging correlates. *Frontiers in Psychology, 7*, 496.

Katz, M. B. (2013). *The Undeserving Poor: America's Enduring \ Confrontation with Poverty.* Fully updated and revised. Oxford University Press.

Kay, J. A., & King, M. A. (2020). *Radical Uncertainty.* Bridge Street Press.

King, A., & Crewe, I. (2014). *The Blunders of our Governments.* Simon and Schuster.

Knight, F. H. (1921). *Risk, Uncertainty and Profit* (Vol. 31). Houghton Mifflin.

Knight, S., Hayhoe, B. W., Frith, L., Ashworth, M., Sajid, I., & Papanikitas, A. (2020). Ethics education and moral decision-making in clinical commissioning: an interview study. *British Journal of General Practice, 70*(690), e45-e54.

Knox, P. (2011). Starchitects, starchitecture and the symbolic capital of world cities. In *International Handbook of Globalization and World Cities.* Edward Elgar Publishing.

Lambert, A. J., Burroughs, T., & Chasteen, A. L. (1998). Belief in a just world and right-wing authoritarianism as moderators of perceived risk. In *Responses to Victimizations and Belief in a Just World* (pp. 107-125). Springer.

Lèfstedt, R. (2011). Department for Work & Pensions. (2011). Reclaiming health and safety for all: An independent review of health and safety legislation. Department for Work & Pensions.

Lerner, M. J., & Simmons, C. H. (1966). Observer's reaction to the "innocent victim": Compassion or rejection?. *Journal of Personality and Social Psychology*, 4(2), 203.

Llorente, J. A. (1843). *The History of the Inquisition of Spain: From the Time of Its Establishment to the Reign of Ferdinand VII. Composed from the Original Documents of the Archives of the Supreme Council and from Those of Subordinate Tribunals of the Holy Office*. James M. Campbell & Company.

Lloyd, E. A., & Oreskes, N. (2018). Climate change attribution: When is it appropriate to accept new methods?. *Earth's Future*, 6(3), 311-325.

MacIntyre, A. (2013). *After Virtue*. A & C Black.

MacIntyre, A. (2019). Doctrine of Double Effect. *The Stanford Encyclopedia of Philosophy*. Edward N. Zalta (Ed.). URL = https://plato.stanford.edu/archives/spr2019/entries/double-effect/

Malthus, T. R., Winch, D., & James, P. (1992). *Malthus: 'An Essay on the Principle of Population'*. Cambridge University Press.

Martin, S. P. (2004). The Radical Necessity Defense. *U. Cin. L. Rev.*, 73, 1527.

Mason, P. (2016). *Postcapitalism: A Guide to our Future*. Macmillan.

McCaul, M. (2016). *Failures of Imagination: The Deadliest Threats to Our Homeland – and how to Thwart Them*. Crown Forum.

McKie, J., & Richardson, J. (2003). The rule of rescue. *Social Science & Medicine*, 56(12), 2407-2419.

Moberly, T. (2017). UK doctors re-examine case for mandatory vaccination. *BMj, 358*, j3414.

Nader, R. (1965). *Unsafe at any Speed: The Designed-in Dangers of the American Automobile*. New York: Grossman.

National Academies of Sciences, Engineering, and Medicine. (2016). *Attribution of Extreme Weather Events in the Context of Climate Change*. National Academies Press.

Nord, E. (1995). The person-trade-off approach to valuing health care programs. *Medical Decision Making, 15*(3), 201-208.

Nozick, R. (1974). *Anarchy, State, and Utopia* (Vol. 5038). New York: Basic Books.

Nussbaum, M. C. (1997). *Poetic Justice: The Literary Imagination and Public Life*. Beacon Press.

Offer, J. (2010). *Herbert Spencer and Social Theory*. Springer.

O'Hara, M. (2016). *Something for Nothing: Arbitrage and Ethics on Wall Street*. WW Norton & Company.

Ottawa, ON, CA.

Percival, R. (2019). The challenge of public law law reform: reflections on a failed Law Commission project. *Journal of Social Welfare and Family Law, 41*(3), 372-383.

Piketty, T. (2018). Capital in the twenty-first century. Harvard University Press.

Pillutla, V., Maslen, H., & Savulescu, J. (2018). Rationing elective surgery for smokers and obese patients: responsibility or prognosis?. *BMC Medical Ethics, 19*(1), 1-10.

Prieto, L., & Sacristán, J. A. (2003). Problems and solutions in calculating quality-adjusted life years (QALYs). *Health and Quality of Life Outcomes, 1*(1), 1-8.

Ragnar, L. (2011). Great Britain Department for Work & Pensions. Reclaiming health and safety for all: An independent review of health and safety legislation.

Rawls, J. (1991). Justice as fairness: Political not metaphysical. In *Equality and Liberty* (pp. 145-173). Palgrave Macmillan, London.

Rawls, J. (2009). *A Theory of Justice*. Harvard University Press.

Rita. In *Volume 3 of the Proceedings of the Futures Working Group*. https://sciences.ucf.edu/fwg/wp-content/uploads/sites/157/2016/11/vol3Jensen.pdf

Ross, D. (2019). Game Theory. *The Stanford Encyclopedia of Philosophy*. Edward N. Zalta (Ed.).

Ruskim, J. (1985). Unto this last and other writings. Penguin.

Sen, A. (1991). Welfare, preference and freedom. *Journal of Econometrics*, *50*(1-2), 15-29.

Sen, A. (1997). *Resources, Values, and Development*. Harvard University Press.

Senior, C. A. (2018). Storylines: an alternative approach to representing uncertainty in physical aspects of climate change. *Climatic Change*, *151*(3-4), 555-571.

Setzer, J., & Byrnes, R. (2019). Global trends in climate change litigation: 2019 snapshot. *Policy Report. URL: www. lse. ac. uk/ GranthamInstitute*.

Shepherd, T. G., Boyd, E., Calel, R. A., Chapman, S. C., Dessai, S., Dima-West, I. M., & Senior, C. A. (2018). Storylines: an alternative approach to representing uncertainty in physical aspects of climate change. *Climatic Change*, *151*(3-4), 555-571.

Shuster, E. (1997). Fifty years later: the significance of the Nuremberg Code. *New England Journal of Medicine*, *337*(20), 1436-1440.

Sinkovics, N., Hoque, S. F., & Sinkovics, R. R. (2016). Rana Plaza collapse aftermath: are CSR compliance and auditing pressures effective?. *Accounting, Auditing & Accountability Journal*, *29*(4), 617-649.

Snow, C. P. (2013). *Science and Government*. Harvard University Press.

Styron, W. (2004). *Sophie's Choice*. Random House.

Sunstein, C. R. (1987). Lochner's legacy. *Colum. L. Rev.*, *87*, 873.

Thomas, P. J., Stupples, D. W., & Alghaffar, M. A. (2006). The Extent of Regulatory Consensus on Health and Safety Expenditure: Part 1: Development of the J-Value Technique and Evaluation of Regulators' Recommendations. Process safety and environmental protection, 84(5), 329-336

Thomas, P. N. (2019). *The Politics of Digital India: Between Local Compulsions and Transnational Pressures*. Oxford University Press.

Thomson, H., & Snell, C. (2013). Quantifying the prevalence of fuel poverty across the European Union. Energy Policy, 52, 563-572.

Thomson, J. J. (1976). Killing, letting die, and the trolley problem. *The Monist*, *59*(2), 204-217.

Tiles, J. E. (1988). *Dewey*. Psychology Press.

Timmins, N., Rawlins, M., & Appleby, J. (2017). A Terrible Beauty: A short history of NICE, the National Institute for Health and Care Excellence. *F1000Research*, 6.

Turner, E. (2017). Berthold Lubetkin:'Nothing is too good for ordinary people'. In *Pioneers in Public Health* (pp. 114-122). Routledge.

UNEP (2015). Climate change and human rights. United Nations Environmental Programme. http://hdl.handle.net/20.500.11822/9530

Urgenda turn the tide?. *Transnational Environmental Law*, 4(2), 339-357.

van Zeben, J. (2015). Establishing a governmental duty of care for climate change mitigation: will Urgenda turn the tide?.

TEL, 4, 339.

Vercher-Chaptal, C. (2018). Limitations and perspectives of responsible management of Global Value Chains: From codes of conduct to the French law on the duty of vigilance. *EURAM 2018*, Jun 2018, Reykjavik, Iceland. <halshs-02141407>

Walzer, M. (2015). *Just and Unjust Wars* (5th edition). Basic Books.

Welsh, J., Thielking, C., & MacFarlane, S. N. (2002). The responsibility to protect: assessing the report of the International Commission on Intervention and State Sovereignty. *International Journal, 57*(4), 489-512.

Williams, A. (2009). 50th anniversary of the 'snob wall' demolition. Oxford Mail: https://www.oxfordmail.co.uk/news/4185278.50th-anniversary-snob-walls-demolition/

World Economic Forum (WEF). (2019). The global risks report 2019. http://www3.weforum.org/docs/WEF_Global_Risks_Report_2019.pdf

 Matador